TRUST THE FLAMES

My Wild Ride from Mindlessness to Mindfulness

KATIE DELIMON

PRAISE FOR *TRUST THE FLAMES*

"*Trust the Flames* is a palate cleanser: a much-needed shot of reality. In a world of highlight reels and curated depictions of life, Katie Delimon assures us that the path to a beautiful life is often a rugged, messy, unfiltered one. Read this memoir."

—**ALICIA COOK,** bestselling poet, award-winning activist and author of *Stuff I've Been Feeling Lately* (Andrews McMeel Publishing 2017) and *Sorry I Haven't Texted You Back* (Andrews McMeel Publishing, 2020)

"While reading *Trust the Flames*, I couldn't stop thinking "I sure wish I'd had this book a decade ago, in my 20s." I was floored by how closely Delimon's experiences, yearnings, mistakes, and insights reflected my own. Never preachy and always engaging *Trust the Flames* feels like a conversation with a big sister or wiser friend who's "been there" and is able to guide you through it with a whole lot of empathy and zero judgment. I truly can't wait to share this with my friends."

—**KAT HAGBERG REBAR** editor, writing coach, and co-author of *Yoga Where You Are* (Shambhala, 2020); editor of *Embodied Resilience Through Yoga* (Llewellyn, 2020); and author of the upcoming *Yoga Inversions* (Shambhala, 2023)

The events and conversations in this book have been set down to the best of the author's ability, although some names and details have been changed to protect the privacy of individuals. Some parts have been fictionalized in varying degrees, for various purposes.

Copyright © 2023 by Kathlyn Delimon

All rights reserved. No part of this book may be reproduced or used in any manner without the written permission of the copyright owner except for the use of quotations in a book review. For more information, email: Katie@katiedelimon.com

First paperback edition February 2023

Cover design by Alice Kurien

Back Cover Photo by Vanda Pap

ISBN 978-0-6454130-0-7 (paperback)
ISBN 978-0-6454130-1-4 (eBook)
ISBN 978-0-6454130-7-6 (hardback)

www.katiedelimon.com

This book is dedicated to my Mamacita

Life is perfect, in its wildness of what it is

Carol-Ann Delimon

INTRODUCTION

We think we meet someone with our eyes, but we actually meet them with our soul.

–Mimi Novic

When I first heard the term "twin flame," I assumed it was just a new, contemporary word for "soulmate;" however, I was mistaken. I learned that—much like a soulmate—a twin flame *is* a person you feel an instant, intense connection with, but there's a unique distinction that sets them apart. The term "soulmate" can mean different things to different people—some will say you can only have one soulmate, while others will say you can have many. In fact, the term has become so ubiquitous that you don't even necessarily need to believe in the concept of souls to believe in soulmates. A "soulmate" can simply refer to someone you immediately jibe with. The definition of a twin flame is a little more specific.

Fair warning: In order to believe in twin flames, you do have to believe in souls that live on after death. That's because the theory of twin flames is based on the idea that at the time of physical death, a soul splits in two, with each half reincarnating as a unique person. This means someone else is carrying the other half of your soul, which is sometimes called a "mirror soul." Because of this mirroring soul component, your twin flame is often a person who is both challenging and healing to you; they will show you your deepest insecurities, fears, and shadows, but they can also help you overcome them (and vice versa).

This memoir reveals my wild adventure from mindlessness to mindfulness, and it also happens to be the story of my twin flame journey. Whether you believe in the concept of twin flames or not, I think you'll be able to relate to a lot of my story, because though it's a spiritual journey, it's also a very human one. And while my experiences and the insights revealed to me may be very different from your own, the themes of love, loss, connection, and desire are integral to the human experience. In sharing my story, and how I ultimately found the life and love I'd been searching for, I hope I'm able to encourage and guide you to uncover an existence that brings your greatest yearnings to fruition. I hope it reminds you that however confusing, heartbreaking, or painful your journey to this point has been, that you can find clarity and peace. That you know a beautiful life is possible—and that you have the power inside you to create it. And that ultimately, you are never alone.

on my NYC balcony aka fire escape

Photo by: Pete Ilosvay

Chapter 1

BURNING OUT

Brooklyn was awake, its volume at full throttle while I cradled my thumping head and buried my face in the sheets. On the street, the noise of someone laying into their car horn while another person's shout rose in an angry crescendo. I dug deeper into the bed, hiding from the slashes of sunlight coming through the blinds.

And then the fuzzy first moments cleared, and I remembered. My mother was in West Virginia.

My mother was dying.

I lifted my head to look at the digital clock on his bedside table. 9:30. I groaned and rolled over. My mouth felt filled with cotton balls. Those Jameson and Gingers seemed like such a good idea when I was dancing in my amethyst bridesmaids' dress. Now they sat heavy in my pounding temples and at the back of my dry throat.

Justin rolled over and opened his big blue eyes. He looked chipper and well-rested, and his perfectly smooth skin didn't show a single wrinkle or blemish, despite the late night and his poor beverage choices. He gave me a quick kiss on the forehead. "Stay here; I'll make you breakfast," he said before jumping out of bed. His energy and lurch from bed only worsened my nausea.

I was numb and awash in guilt. Justin was crazy-sweet. My mom loved him. Everyone loved Justin. I should have felt like the luckiest girl in the world to have him for a boyfriend.

I didn't feel lucky at all, though. It was wrong to feel good in Brooklyn while my mom was miles away, fighting for her life.

Justin rummaged through the pots and pans searching for the right one. I snaked my hand out from under the covers, fumbled for my iPhone and swiped it on. It was the first of the month – time for my monthly horoscope by astrologist queen and fellow Pisces, Susan Miller.

I first read Susan's work two years earlier. She had a column in a magazine that I'd won a copy of after stripping down to my underpants at a trendy bookstore in Sydney, Australia. No, I'm not insane. It was a competition. I cheated by wearing a pair of men's black boxer briefs, and they initially tried to deny me my prize. These days, anything that reminded me of Australia, including Susan Miller, held a special place in my heart.

I tapped the Safari icon and typed in astrologyzone.com. The page slowly loaded but the day's horoscopes weren't posted yet. That's weird, Susan is so devoted, I thought to myself. I scrolled further down the page and found a blog post titled "Little Mom." My breath caught in my throat. I referred to my mother as "Mamacita," which is Spanish for "little mom." The post was a letter dedicated to Susan Miller's mother whose funeral was being held that day, hence the absent horoscopes. I shivered from the synchronicity and continued to read.

She said her "little mom" was watching from heaven and signed it off with a loving tribute about her love as wide as the world and deep as the ocean. A love that would go on forever in her heart.

The screen on my phone went black. "Home" was calling. It was my "faja," my dad. (I had been calling my dad "Faja" since the movie *Austin Powers: Goldmember* came out as an inside joke, referencing how the so-called villain pronounced the word "father.")

Nausea and a jolt of heat thrummed through my entire body, leaving me cold and shaking. I didn't want to take this call, but I slid my thumb to the right and answered anyway. My Dad's face appeared on the screen.

"Hey, Faja." My voice sounded like I was speaking underwater through a mouthful of stones. I noticed how pale my face looked in the tiny box next to my dad's image, but I did nothing about it.

"Hey, Kate," my dad said. There was a slight pause, and I heard him draw a ragged breath. "Mommy didn't have a good night last night."

Everything stopped. All sound, all air. I had the constant sick feeling of freefall. Time stopped.

My dad paused again, and the dread solidified in my belly like a rock.

"She died this morning."

I had never seen my dad cry, but I could tell by his voice that despite their fraught history, he'd just lost a piece of himself. For a single hopeful moment, it struck me: *I'm still dreaming. This can't be real. I'm asleep.*

I struggled to remain calm, fighting back the tears. "All right. Thank you for calling, Faja. I love you. I'll be down later today," I said, running the words together in a rush to get them out before I lost control.

"OK," he said. "Please be careful. Drive safe. Take your time and don't rush. I love you."

"I love you too, Dad."

That was the first time my dad told me he loved me with those words. Usually, I say I love you and he will answer, "Okay, honey; me too." I'd always wanted to hear those words but today, more than anything, they just brought home the truth: my mom was gone.

∼

Mom was dead, and I was hungover in a home that wasn't mine, with a man I didn't love, in a life that felt…wrong. I had been burning out for a long time. But this day, as awful as it was, wasn't when it all started. If anything, it was the start of the undoing.

My mom had a favorite quote by the writer Hunter S. Thompson:

"Life should not be a journey to the grave with the intention of arriving safely in a pretty and well-preserved body, but rather to skid in broadside in a cloud of smoke, thoroughly used up, totally worn out, and loudly proclaiming, 'Wow! What a ride!'"

I had taken this quote literally for the past 26 years. And the ride was about to get even bumpier.

Chapter 2

WILDFIRES

It was almost midnight. I was walking home along the waterfront to my new apartment in Bondi after leaving work at Hurricanes. I still couldn't believe that I was living here at 23 years old – among young, Australian beach-goers in one of the most beautiful and iconic parts of the world. I breathed in the salt air. I didn't even mind wearing dirty black stretch pants that smelt of Hurricane's famous rib sauce.

It was the last call at the Beach Road Hotel and drunk people were stumbling out, arms wrapped around each other, laughing. A bike bell rang from behind me, and I jumped out of the way, thinking about the beach cruiser Mom was bringing when she flew over in a few weeks. I was still unsure how we would get along while she was here, but I was cautiously optimistic.

The bell rang again and two guys passed me. "Thank you," they called as they passed.

Suddenly I found myself shouting back. "You're welcome. Hey, I like your bell. Where did you get it?"

I cringed immediately and would cringe for years whenever I thought of it. Who blurts out compliments to strangers about their bike bells?

The tall one stopped pedaling and turned around. His mountain bike matched his dark hair and black t-shirt.

"This old thing?" he said. "I can't remember. You can get them anywhere they sell bikes, I'm sure."

His friend pulled up short as well. With blonde hair, hazel eyes and black square-framed prescription glasses, he rode a more petite, silver BMX that suited his stature. He also didn't look too impressed to be stopping.

The tall Australian continued, "So, are you walking back from Beach Road?" He let the bike lean between his legs and held it casually with one hand by the handlebars.

"No, I just left work at Hurricanes. I'm headed home."

"Ah, they have the best ribs ever," he said. "Where do you live?"

I remember being taken aback. Australians weren't usually so forward. I paused for a second before deciding to make a joke out of it.

"I just met you guys. I don't even know your names. Why would I tell you where I lived?"

He laughed. "Ah c'mon," he said. "It's not like that. My name is John. This is my roommate Finn. We were just at the Beach Road and we live in North Bondi on Owen St. I'm just asking so that we can make sure you get home safe."

I looked them over. John seemed nice. He was a bit older and had, so far, been polite and respectful. His roommate Finn still hadn't said anything, but he seemed OK and very cute. And anyway, this is how you meet people in Bondi.

"I just live on Onslow Street in Rose Bay," I said.

John said, "Well our place is on the way. Why don't you come by for a drink? Then one of us can walk you home."

"Sure, why not," I said. My mom always told me to trust my intuition and so I did.

Their place wasn't far and when we got there, we piled into the small living room. I took my shoes off and felt immediately at home. John played DJ and we listened to the Supremes.

We started talking and Finn came out of his shell. It didn't take me long to switch my focus to Finn—John was great, but Finn was exactly my type.

"Are you from the UK?" I asked. He had a strong British accent, but with a touch of something I hadn't recognized.

"Sort of," he said. "I'm from Sweden, but I moved to the UK when I was young."

"How long have you been here then?"

"Only about five years," he said.

I laughed. "Only? I've *only* been here about three months!"

Finn and John both laughed. "It sounds long when you put it that way."

"Why'd you come to Australia?" John asked. He was squatting on the floor across the room, his dark hair like a shadow thrown across the wall.

"I've always wanted to visit," I said. "You ever get that feeling you're exactly where you're supposed to be?"

Finn laughed. I could tell he didn't get it. I shifted on the couch to get more comfortable, and as I did my knee brushed against his briefly. I surprised myself by blushing.

I glanced up to see John watching us and blushed a deeper pink.

"Why does anyone do anything?" I said. "Why does the earth spin around? Why does falling hurt? Why do people fall in love?" Ugh. More memories for the cringe file.

But Finn was looking thoughtful. "I get it," he said, shooting me a big smile, and I felt myself glow from the inside out. I don't remember, but I'm sure I blushed again. "I've travelled all over the world just because I wanted to be in a certain place at a specific time. And it's worked out well for me so far."

"Where have you been?" I asked. Now we were moving into my favorite topic. I love travel stories and the new information I glean adds to my growing list of places I want to visit.

Finn started speaking to me about the places he'd been in Europe. Every time he mentioned some place I'd been to or wanted to go, I'd interrupt and we'd talk about what we loved about it, the things we'd done or wished we'd done differently next time. I'd had many conversations like this even with other 'backpackers' in Bondi, but this felt different. It wasn't just a conversation. It felt like our souls were conversing.

John changed the music. Michael Jackson rolled out of the speakers. Finn reached into his pocket, pulled out a packet and rolled a cigarette.

"I didn't know people rolled cigarettes; what year are we in?" I asked.

He laughed. "Don't knock it till you try it."

So, I said, "Roll one for me, too?"

With the paper in his left hand, he sprinkled tobacco with his right and, in a single deft movement, rolled a perfect cigarette without breaking eye contact. He smiled as he presented the finished product and said, "let's smoke." Sydney is warm in

October, but the night still holds the last crispness of spring. As we stepped out into the backyard, I trembled in my t-shirt.

"Are you cold?" Finn asked.

"A little," I laughed. Finn went inside and brought back a black and white striped sweater that fit like a glove. I loved it immediately.

The night was finally quiet in a way that Bondi only is after the bars shut down and before the early morning exercising begins. Our conversations meandered and when Finn got pictures of him scuba diving, John excused himself to bed, but we barely noticed.

We got deep and personal pretty fast. I found myself opening up to him in a way I hadn't for a long time, telling him things I tried to hide from most people. Things that I felt so much shame around like my family and my past.

He talked about his mom, brothers, stepdad and what it was like to move to Australia alone. His stories zigzagged from the past to the present, across continents, cities and what felt like lifetimes. I was smitten, whether it was the Australian night or my electric currents. Like a magnet, I was utterly drawn to him.

A travelling nomad not exactly sure where he is from with a colorful childhood and an adopted brother. I could relate to it all, more than with anyone else I'd ever met.

"It's 2:30," Finn said. "You've got to get up for work soon. We'd better get you home."

"Yeah, all right," I said, but I really, *really* didn't want the night to end.

Finn walked me home through silent streets. In the distance, we could hear the ocean. He had his hands tucked deep into the pockets of his jeans and a grey hoodie pulled up over his head. The closer my apartment got, the more I didn't want him to go.

We got to the front door. "Come up," I said. "My roommate isn't home." I laughed a little to offset how vulnerable I felt. In my head, I repeated *Just come up. Come up.*

He gave a little nod and headed up the stairs. My heart lurched as I followed him. Inside we chatted for a minute but it's the kind of nonsense that you're saying when you're thinking about something else. And we were both thinking about what was going to come next. Finally, Finn stood up and came over to me. He was the perfect height for leaning in for a kiss. It was soft and gentle at first, but soon it became electric. I knew he felt the same and as the kiss increased in urgency, we half stumbled, half weaved our way to the bedroom and onto the bed. *Yes!* Heat flushed through my entire body.

Things escalated quickly and before I knew it, I was whispering "yes, yes" into his ear and we were making love. We fit together perfectly; it was what I hoped for and more.

We hardly slept and were running on sheer adrenaline as dawn came in through the window blinds. There was no awkwardness or shame. We shared that fantastic feeling you get after something momentous has happened.

Finn offered to drive me to work. It was quicker than taking the bus and we could stay in bed longer. When we got to the restaurant, he didn't just drop me at the curb, but he parked the car and walked me up to the front door.

"I had a great night," Finn said.

I smiled. "Me too."

"Are you busy tonight? Do you want to hang out?" he asked.

"Yeah. I get off at 6 pm," I said. And that was it. I realized as I walked into work that I felt surprised. And also like I was dreaming. Who was this guy who could so easily say what he wanted without playing games? Could it really be this easy?

It really was that easy, at least in the beginning.

After that first night, Finn and I were a couple. We spent as much time as we could together. Each morning when it came time to say goodbye Finn would ask, "Are you busy tonight?" until he no longer had to ask. We flowed into each other's lives quickly and painlessly, merging our groups of friends at parties and events together.

He would meet me after work and we'd walk hand-in-hand along the foreshore to meet friends at the Beach or The Bondi Hotel. We'd have quiet nights in, ordering Thai food, watching movies or listening to music while we caught up on our day. Even better, he met my mom and Aunt Denise when they visited. They drank Australian ciders and watched as Finn helped put my pearlescent beach cruiser together in the living room.

I spent Christmas and New Year's with his family when they visited from England. We ate boiled Christmas puddings—an English tradition—prawns—an Aussie tradition—and even pecan pie—an American southern specialty, and laughed about the unique Christmas lunch combination we'd created.

It was convenient that we lived just blocks from each other, but I saw this as serendipitous. And I loved that we cared about the same things in life. Travelling, spending time with friends and anything involving the ocean. Finn loved to surf and I loved the sun so living on the world's biggest island was perfect for us.

Soon we fulfilled our dream of traveling together. Our adoration of the ocean took us to a smaller island off the coast of Australia…Fiji. We spent two weeks exploring, scuba diving with bull sharks (without a cage), snorkeling with manta rays on Manta Ray Island and soaking up the warm, friendly Fijian vibes. Bula!

But some of the best times we spent together were the most unremarkable. Late afternoons on the beach we'd talk about our lives while seawater dried on our skin leaving faint lines of salt. Late afternoon beers at the local pub where the bartenders knew us by name. Weekend getaways. We were as together as two people could be. Aligned.

For nine months, we were inseparable. We laughed when we were together and infused everything we did with fun. We were *in love*. But there was a ticking clock. My time in Australia was nearing its end. And the only way I could extend my visa was if I decided to go on a student visa or if Finn and I were engaged.

I contemplated the student visa option but it felt too restrictive. I didn't want to go back to school and there were limits to how much I could work. Plus, I still had my American college student loan to pay off. I didn't feel ready to add to my debt with an Australian student loan.

We thought about the engagement option, but it came with a significant catch—you had to marry within a year. It felt too forced. We were in love, but we didn't want to feel pressured into marriage by anything or anyone.

None of the options felt right.

Toward the end, the pressure of deciding our future caused a lot of friction between us. Everything felt out of my control. It was impossible to know what would happen after I left. Inside me was a daunting knowledge that our relationship had an expiry date, but I was too stubborn to accept defeat.

I started to notice familiar tendencies creeping in, like excessive sleeping of 12 or more hours a day, low energy, not having an appetite and losing weight. And after a few too many drinks, fights would bubble to the surface. My alter ego of anger and dissociation would make me unlikable to be around with snide, snarky remarks personally directed at Finn or emotionally detaching from dealing with emotional issues altogether.

During my final weeks in Sydney, things weren't going well between Finn and me, but on my last night, something happened that left me with a glimmer of hope.

Finn made us a reservation for dinner. All I knew was that it was somewhere near the harbor and that I was to dress nice. So, I put on my rose-colored tube top dress, layered for Sydney's winter with black tights, a black leather jacket, a cream pashmina scarf and four-inch patent leather ankle booties. I paired this with a way too freshly sprayed fake tan because there was no way I was going back to the States pale in the middle of summer after spending a year in Australia.

Finn looked handsome in black pants, a white button-up shirt and a classic black skinny tie with his black square prescription glasses. The taxi ride over to the restaurant was bittersweet. We held hands and sat closely together, quietly talking about nothing as the city swept past. I felt aware of every passing second.

It was a strange contrast—the normalcy of the city and all the people in it going about their lives, underpinned by the sweet pain of the looming separation. I clutched onto him, memorizing the shape of his hand in mine and watching the lights flash over his skin. I wanted to remember everything.

When we got to the harbor, Finn paid for the taxi and then reached out a hand to help me out of the car. As I stood, I pulled him in for a hug. I didn't want to let go. Ever.

Finn chuckled. "We'll miss our reservation, Katie." He pulled back. "Come on, the night's young. It's not over yet." I wanted to share his happiness for the evening, but all I could feel was yearning.

We walked into the restaurant together and headed up the wooden staircase toward another seating area where I saw fifteen of my closest Sydney friends jump up and yell, "*Surprise!*"

I was stunned and began to cry. I felt overwhelmed with love, joy and sadness all wrapped up into one. I had never had a surprise before and it felt good to feel so loved.

Wine and seafood flowed all night. It was perfect. Everyone told stories, reminiscing and making plans to come and visit me in the States. I had Finn by my side, who was at his best, cracking jokes, paying me compliments and charming all our friends. I wished for that night never to end.

As the evening was wrapping up (the restaurant staff looking impatient as they waited for us to depart), Finn gave me two parting gifts.

"OK, OK," he said. "Before everyone rolls out of here, I have something I want to do." He smiled at me, his eyes directly looking into mine, and my stomach lurched. "So everyone knows Katie leaves tomorrow, and no one is more upset to see her go than me. And while I don't think she will go off and forget me, I wanted to give her a little something to remember me and us."

He reached behind him and pulled out a brown-wrapped package. My hands shook as I opened it to find a framed picture of us that he had created. When you looked at it from one angle we were smiling and then when you looked at it from the other angle, we were making silly faces. Everyone at the table oohed and aahed.

"Finn! I love it," I said. "Thank you so much! I don't know when you did this!"

Finn said, "I had to sneak around. But it was worth it, right?"

"Definitely. Definitely." I smiled down at our picture. The two of us making goofy faces.

"But I'm not done," Finn said. "Just one more thing." He reached into his pocket and pulled out another package, which was much smaller. He handed it to me, his eyes never leaving my face.

"Another one. This is too much, really" I said. My heart was pounding and I could feel the hot blush from my face creeping down my neck. I took the package from him and tore into the wrapping. As it came away, I heard a sharp tinkle sound. It was the original bell off of John's bike. I turned it over in my hand, looking at the old metal glinting in the soft light of the restaurant.

"Katie, no one knows the future," Finn said, "but on the day you first asked about this bell and we met, I felt my future begin." Tears rushed to my eyes, and as I looked around at all my friends I thought, *was this really happening?*

Finn reached down and took my hand. "Even though you're leaving tomorrow, I hope you know this isn't the end for us. And this bell is that promise. We still have our future." He leaned across and gave me a soft kiss and I felt like my heart would explode. Everything was going to be OK after all, despite the worry and angst of the past few weeks. I wasn't sure if the bell was a promise ring but it certainly left the impression on my friends and me that this was the real deal.

Maybe someone should have pinched me and woken me up from the dream. But I doubt I would have woken. Finn was that all-consuming love that affects and infects everything in your life. The kind you don't feel at the time you could survive its loss. With Finn, I couldn't even bear to consider an alternate reality. Instead, I focused on keeping this reality together at all costs, no matter the consequences.

But I was to only realize this later with hindsight. At the time, I was putting everything I had into our relationship. I was burning hard and fast. We weren't tending to each other but were fueling each other's fire.

∼

The following day as I was waiting for my flight, Finn and I hugged in front of the big yellow block letters that spelled "DEPARTURES" at Sydney International airport. I could feel my body shuddering against him, his arms wrapped around me, holding me firmly. I was devastated. Utterly devastated.

Finn finally pulled back and held me at arms-length. I looked into his hazel eyes, red from crying.

"I'll see you soon," he said, even though neither of us knew when soon would come. I wanted to believe somehow that we had a future together but doing so took more faith than I had at the time. A voice came over the public address system to announce my flight while tears ran down my cheeks. I wanted to believe him, but in my gut, I couldn't.

Were we ready to make the kind of commitment required with such a distance between us? I feared what wasn't guaranteed once I stepped on that plane. But I had no choice. My visa had ended. I had to go home.

I cried so much for the first hour to California that the guy next to me asked if I was OK and offered some tissues.

"Thanks, I'm OK,' I said, but I kept my blue Wayfarer's on and pretended to sleep. My thoughts were racing. "What if I never go back? What if I never see him again? What if he meets someone else?"

Mamacita, me & Denise
— Hunter Valley, AU

Dear Katie, 11-12-09

I had a wonderful time. I know we don't spend much time alone together, but it meant alot to me just being here with you. I want you to enjoy the rest of your time away from home, just be sure to come home. This is too far away. I Love you with all my heart and will keep you in my thoughts until you come home. If you need anything you know you can just ask. Be safe, be happy. Love Always & Forever, Mamacita xoxoxo

I will explore this amazing place again some time in the future. So much to see.

with Amanda in our apt.
445 78th St.

Photo by: Pete Iloskvay

Chapter 3

FLAMING FRONT

I left a big piece of my heart in Australia, but I was also heading back to fulfill one of my other childhood dreams – to live in New York City, sharing an apartment with my very best friend, Amanda. So, even though I was sad about leaving Finn and uncertain about our relationship, I was also excited to embark on my new life. As the planet unrolled beneath the plane, I slowly looked forward instead of back.

Landing at Newark airport was almost as surreal as leaving Sydney. Within hours, I was on the PATH train headed into the City. It was all so normal; it was almost like I'd never left. I felt my body relax into the familiar sway of the train as it moved along the tracks. It felt good to be home, but I couldn't stop worrying about what I'd left behind.

I would meet Amanda at the French Connection store in Soho where she was now the store manager. When I arrived at the corner of Broadway and Prince Street, I pulled the heavy glass door toward me and felt a rush of cool air. Amanda was at the counter – her long, thick brown hair and perpetually tanned skin were hard to miss. Italian through and through.

I must have still been emotional from the flight and my goodbyes to Finn because as soon as I saw Amanda, I started to tear up. I brushed the tears away quickly, but not before she noticed.

She pushed out from behind the counter and pulled me into a big hug.

"Oh, Scrum! It's so good to see you." The first night we met we were in a basement dive bar, Down the Hatch, in Greenwich Village, when some random guy asked for our names and she blurted out, "My name is Delicious and this is my friend, Scrumptious." This became our alias so we never had to give our real names. We still call each other Delish and Scrum for short. She pulled back to have a look at me.

"Oh my god, you're withering away. Where'd you go?"

I shrugged. I had lost 30 pounds since I'd left New Jersey and gone to Australia. I hadn't been trying to lose weight, but between long hours working and long hours spent with Finn, I hadn't spent too much time eating.

Amanda studied me carefully. You can't hide from a good friend; she could see I was having trouble speaking. I was afraid I'd start to cry again.

"C'mon," she said. "I want to show you the apartment." She flung her arm around me and steered me toward the entrance. With Amanda, it was always life to the fullest. When she wanted to show you an apartment, she wanted to show you now. I love that about her.

The apartment was on the corner of 79th and York. When we walked up the humid stairway and saw the dark green door with the skewed 4A on the front, I knew I was home. My heart wanted this so badly. I would find a job and do whatever I had to do to make it work.

Amanda swung the door open. Directly in front of the door was a bathroom the size of a closet. It just fits a sink, a bathtub, and a toilet with space left over for no more than one person. Past the bathroom was the kitchen. If you stood in the middle of the kitchen, you could touch everything without moving your feet. Beyond the kitchen was the first bedroom, which would be mine. It had no windows. Four feet further down the hall was Amanda's room. It was bigger, not by much, but it did have two large windows and the fire escape, aka a New York City balcony, meaning this was prime real estate. There was no living room. It was tiny, but it was perfect.

After the 10-second tour, we walked back into the kitchen.

"De-liiish," I said, "I love it. Where are the closets? I didn't see any?"

Amanda looked at me, startled, her eyes wide. Then we both just started cracking up. She was wheezing and I was literally holding my sides. We were laughing so hard.

"Oh my god, I didn't even realize. How did I not notice there were no closets? What's wrong with me?"

That just made us laugh harder. Thirty-six hours earlier, I was crying in my boyfriend's arms in Sydney, Australia, and now I was dying of laughter with my best friend on the floor of an empty apartment in New York City. Maybe things would be OK after all.

"So, do you think you'll move in?" she asked as we struggled to catch our breath.

"Oh my god, are you kidding me? Of course! Abso – fucking – lutely!" I said. "I just need a week or two to get my shit together."

I was ecstatic to live in New York City with Amanda but still felt like a piece of the puzzle missing, 10,000 miles away.

～

He's here, he's here! I sang over and over in my mind. It had been three months since I had seen Finn and one year since we met. We were flying into San Francisco, me from New York City and him from Sydney. When we saw each other, it was magic. Finn seemed just as happy and excited to see me as I was him.

We'd rented a silver convertible Ford Mustang to drive down the Pacific Coast Highway to Los Angeles and eventually to Las Vegas. I sat next to Finn with the top down and the ocean air swirling around us. We would stop when we got hungry and eat sandwiches in little cafes in picturesque towns along the way, taking photos from the cliff tops overlooking the Pacific Ocean – the same ocean that was there when we met on the other side of the world. We explored The Monterey Bay Aquarium, Joshua Tree, Monument Valley, The Grand Canyon and my favorite, Antelope Canyon.

I believed that life couldn't get more perfect. Finn was here. We were finally together and going to embrace everything life had to offer.

Having Finn in my life, *really* in my life, felt right, but there was also an undercurrent of worry buzzing below the surface at all times. Where was this going? How could we keep it going when we lived on opposite sides of the world?

After Vegas we flew to see family in West Virginia and when we arrived, Finn got some surprising news from his company back in Sydney.

"Katie, my boss told me there's room for me to transfer from our Sydney office to our New York office. If I want it," Finn said.

I sat up from my childhood bedroom where I'd been dozing.

"What? Really?" I asked.

"Yep," Finn smiled. "I mean it's not set in stone or anything, but it's a real possibility."

"Oh my god," I said, throwing my arms around his neck. His hair was still damp from the shower and smelled of orange Dial soap. "That's incredible!"

Inside I felt something that was wound up start to unravel. The relief was physical. Finally, something that made sense. A way for us to be together without having to rush marriage or go back to school. Plus, Finn would be coming to New York City. A place I wasn't ready to leave yet.

I remember telling my mom the news and she was relieved too. Australia was just a little bit too far away for her liking. She loved it and thought it was a beautiful country but I knew if it were up to her, she would have preferred me to be closer. Much closer.

We started making plans. Finn would return to Australia for a few months and then come to the States. We'd spend a few years in New York City, then move back to Australia. We had a plan, a legitimate plan. So, when it came time to say goodbye at the airport, I didn't sob this time. I left with a sense of hope rather than uncertainty.

Unfortunately, it wasn't to last.

whitewater Rafting trip WV

Chapter 4

FUEL LOAD

After Finn left, I moved into a state of limbo. I managed to get an interview for a corporate job, though I had yet to hear anything definite. I was happy in New York City but at the same time, I felt like my life was on pause until I knew when Finn would be moving to the states.

Instead of progress, we digressed. I was getting antsy, pressing Finn to give me more concrete plans when he couldn't. Each week we grew further apart. On the phone, we fought over the small stuff. Finding that natural flow between us was hard when everything had to be so planned out. Sure, the time difference was hard, but it was only a month after he left that our relationship truly got tested.

It was just before Thanksgiving, and New York City had that melancholy look that it gets in the winter. People hurry along icy streets in black coats, and the concrete buildings appear to hunker down along the skyline. I pushed open the door to French Connection, where I was now the assistant store manager alongside Amanda and as I was in the middle of peeling off my frozen scarf and gloves, my phone rang.

"Hi Aunt Rose," I said, opening my red flip phone while trying to pull off my other glove at the same time.

"Hey Kate," Rose said. I knew immediately that something was wrong. She didn't call me "Doodle," her nickname for me. Her voice was subdued and quiet, not her typical bubbly tone.

"Your mom's in the hospital. She was sick this morning and couldn't even walk from her car to the door at work." Her voice caught at the end of the sentence.

The room shrank around me. "What happened?" I asked. "I know she had a cough. Did it get worse?" My mom had gotten sick after we all jumped in the river white water rafting last month when Finn was visiting. She thought it was just a cold.

"I took her straight to the hospital," Rose said. "It turns out that one side of her lungs had filled up with liquid and collapsed." Rose took a deep breath, 'So she had to go in for surgery. They glued the lining of her lung back to her chest."

"OK," I said. My jacket felt much too hot now that I was inside, but I couldn't gather the will to take it off. "Is she alright? How's she doing?" My words barely came out.

"Yes, she's OK. The surgery went well." Rose paused and I heard the sound of West Virginia in the background – the birds squeaking in the trees and the ping of the old oil heater in Aunt Rose's living room.

She continued, "But they found cancer cells in the liquid on her lungs."

The world fell silent. I could hear the blood pounding in my ears. *My mom had cancer.* My strong, vibrant mom had cancer. How could that be? She was only 53.

"Do they know what kind, the diagnosis, next steps?" I asked finally. I looked down at my hand, white-knuckled on the counter's edge. I'd forgotten where I was.

"Look honey, we aren't sure about a lot of things and we're still waiting for results to come back. We'll see what the doctors say after more tests tomorrow."

"All right. Well, it's Thanksgiving on Thursday, should I drive down?" In my head, I was already packing. A feeling of hopelessness overwhelmed me, and I was grasping for something, anything to do.

"Yes. I think that would be good," Rose said. "Your brother Rob is coming up from Virginia too and your mom will be in the hospital for a few more days. It'd be nice for her to see you."

I closed my phone. I looked around the store. Everything was the same. The same racks of clothes. The same staff talking to customers. The same counter and till, the one I was leaning on. But somehow, everything was utterly different. *My mom had cancer.*

I said the words in my head. But I still didn't understand how they could be real.

The day dragged on. I longed to crawl out of my skin. I kept looking at my phone expecting it to be almost time to clock off, only to find that 10 minutes had passed. When I finally made it home, I threw off my gloves, scarf and jacket, sat in our tiny kitchen and logged onto Skype to call Finn. I felt lost and scared, desperate for reassurance.

The video was fuzzy. I could only just make out Finn against a blur of broken pixels.

My throat felt hot and painful like it was closing up so it was difficult to breathe. My eyes filled with tears. "Where are you

Finn, where are you? And why is it so hard getting a hold of you?" I said, unable to stifle a sob.

"I am here to talk and listen but you need to be realistic about when we can call." His voice was fading in and out, but not enough to disguise the edge of impatience in his tone. The space between us felt wider than the Pacific Ocean. I'd blamed our time difference and the literal distance. Maybe it was more.

I brushed the tears away. My cheeks stung from being rubbed raw. I tried to pull it together, but everything that I was feeling came out in a rush and my voice sounded like a raw howl.

"I just don't feel like I'm a priority in your life."

I put my head in my hands and cried. On the other side of the world, Finn shrugged. "I don't know what I can do," he said.

From that night on, the distance between us grew. The silences became longer. It became harder and harder to pin Finn down about anything. It was the start of summer in Australia, but winter in New York, so he was out more and I was in more.

He was becoming cagey about his potential move to the States, and I found myself needing to convince him. Whenever I brought it up, he'd brush it aside with a quick "Can we not talk about this right now?" before changing the subject. I didn't sense enthusiasm. It was clear that I was not going to make any moves back to Australia while my mom was unwell. So, we were stuck. My instinct was he didn't want to move but he couldn't come right out and tell me. It was difficult to accept. I couldn't bear the thought of our relationship ending.

A few days later I went to see my mom in the hospital in West Virginia. She was sitting up in bed when I came in, organizing all the receipts in her purse. She looked so much like herself – so solid and real – but sick and tired, of course, and the IVs and the monitors snaking from her arm and the sounds and smells of the hospital made the diagnosis seem so real. I was grown up, I'd travelled the world, I wasn't afraid of much. But seeing my mom like this made me feel small, like a child again.

My mom turned to look at me and a huge smile bloomed across her face. I felt the heaviness release a little in my chest. She was still my mom. And despite our sometimes-complicated relationship, I loved her. She pulled me into a mom hug, and for a brief moment, everything felt all right.

Later I went into the hallway to grab a cup of coffee from those horrible vending machines. I was ducking down to grab what was supposed to be a cappuccino but it looked more like tepid pond water when I saw my brother Rob walking toward me. He had his chin tucked and his head down, so I only saw the top of his gorgeous big brown head and the slump of his shoulders. He looked up and our eyes met.

The floodgates opened. I could barely stand. I set my cup down carefully as I sunk to the floor and buried my face in my hands. Rob came up and put his arm around me. He smelled like his familiar cologne, Fahrenheit. It made me cry more.

"It's going to be OK," he said. His voice was soft but firm.

"Is it?" I asked. "I was such a bitch toward her and I feel like I've always been so angry and resentful. What if I never get the chance to treat her better?" I was sobbing and snuffling, surprised Rob could even understand me.

"We were all like that as kids," he said. "That's just adolescence. Mommy knows that. She loves you." He patted my back gently as we sat on the hall floor. People were walking past but nobody paid too much attention. It was the cancer ward, after all.

We met with the doctors. They hadn't been able to find cancer anywhere else in her body, so she was diagnosed with lung cancer. Strange because she didn't have any lung tumors and she hadn't smoked a cigarette in over 25 years. We wanted her to get a second opinion but she accepted the diagnosis and so we had to, as well. They scheduled her first chemo appointment for just before Christmas.

I didn't want to leave, but my mom wanted me to.

"You have to live your life, Katie," she said. "I'm fine. Just fine." She paused and squeezed my hand, her eyes locked on mine. "You have your big new job, your new apartment in Manhattan and Amanda. I don't want you to miss out on any of that."

"I know, but what if you need me?"

"Then I can call you. You can be here in no time. Really, honey. I want you to keep living your life. There's so much out there for you."

With some people, this might have just sounded like the *right* thing to say. But I knew my mom meant it. She'd always lived her life on her terms. She did what she wanted, when she wanted because it felt authentic. She loved her family. A part of her still loved my dad. But she also chose herself first. And she was asking me to do the same. So, I packed up my bags and drove eight hours back home to New York City.

Chapter 5

IGNITED

Sunday morning. One of those cold winter mornings in New York where the clouds are grey and snow is swirling in the sky. I'd been back in the City for a week. I hadn't heard from Finn, and it didn't surprise me. This had become our pattern.

I popped out of bed and grabbed my laptop, quickly swinging back under the covers before losing all the warmth. The heat was on, but I was shivering, my fingers skittered over the keyboard. The Facebook inbox opened, and I was thrilled to see a new mail message from someone in Sydney… but it wasn't a message from Finn.

If you think your boyfriend has been faithful, think again.

I squeezed my eyes shut, my heart pounding. *I must have read that wrong.* I opened them again, frantically scanning the short message over and over.

If you think your boyfriend has been faithful, think again.

No matter how many times I read it, it said the same thing.

I wanted to believe it was a lie – a message sent by someone out of spite or jealousy. But in my heart, in my soul, I knew it was true.

I rolled out of my bed and ran into Amanda's room. She was asleep curled around her Boston terrier, chihuahua, and pug mix, Bella. They looked so peaceful, but I needed her.

"Delish, wake up. Finn cheated on me," I said. Amanda's eyes flew open. She struggled to sit up.

"What?" she said. "What are you talking about?" She slowly sat up, brushing her long hair back from her face. Bella grunted and rolled over. My message didn't have the same effect on the pup.

"I got a message. Some girl in Sydney sent me a message." I collapsed onto her bed and pulled Bella to me. Her rough fur and warm body offered comfort.

"Wait, tell me exactly what the message said," Amanda said.

I brought my computer in to show her though it didn't take long to analyze the message.

"Don't freak out yet," Amanda said, "you don't know what happened. Wait till you talk to Finn."

Of course, she was right. She was always my voice of reason. I tried to ring Finn, but he didn't answer. I tried Skype and sent text messages, but they all went unanswered. With every minute, my stomach sank further, and dread mounted.

That day, I felt like a plastic bag drifting through the wind. I got ready for work on autopilot, pulling clothes out of my plastic container drawers at random. I got through the day with no idea what I was doing, what I was saying, or even what I was selling. Customers looked at me oddly when I was showing them clothes or ringing them up, and I realized that I must be doing it all wrong, but I couldn't be bothered to care. I went through the motions without control. Every fiber of my being was focused on Finn.

Where is he? Why isn't he responding? Who is this other girl? He's probably not responding because it's true. What if he ends it with no explanation?

I felt like that crazy girlfriend. And I literally could not help myself. I had to speak to him.

It took me half a day to get a hold of Finn, which felt like the longest 12 hours of my life. By the time I reached him, it was the late evening for me. I was already a bottle of wine and half a pack of cigarettes in.

When he picked up, he was carefully nonchalant, as if he hadn't seen the torrent of unanswered communications that I'd been hurtling his way. "Hey, babe. What's up?" he said. It was quiet in the background.

"Finn, did you cheat on me?" I asked. My voice shook. My whole body felt like it was shaking.

He was quiet so I filled the silence.

"I got a message from someone saying you haven't been faithful. I don't know who the girl is but why would she write me a message like that?"

Still no reply. I felt my heart pounding in my chest. I had my answer. I already knew.

Finally, he spoke. "Yes, and I was going to tell you but I didn't think it was a good time."

A good time? No, you're right. It's probably not the best time for me but when is it EVER a good time to be told you were cheated on?

I should be shouting that from the rooftops, but I was so angry, so sick, so absolutely and utterly *sad*.

"I don't think it's ever a "good time," Finn," I said. "Who is she? When did it happen, *where* did it happen?" *Oh, God, not his bed!* "Just tell me what exactly happened?"

I didn't want to hear the details, but I couldn't help myself. I had to know everything. And now that it was out in the open, Finn was willing to talk.

"It was just a girl from work… at the Christmas party. All we did was kiss. I swear. That's it."

"What does this mean?" I asked. "Are you seeing her?"

"No, she has a boyfriend, too," he said. *As if that means anything. It didn't stop them in the first place.* "It was just a drunken thing."

I closed my eyes. The tears were still coursing down my face. The worst had happened.

I wanted a name, but he wouldn't give it to me. No matter what I said or how many different ways I asked. Not that it mattered. This hurt. This was personal – a blow to my ego. *Am I not a good enough girlfriend? Am I not a good enough person? I must have done something wrong to have caused this otherwise it wouldn't have happened. Is this the only rational explanation? Do I blame myself?*

"Katie?" Finn said, the unasked question hanging in the air.

"I need some time to think," I said. I couldn't imagine ending it, even now.

"Of course," he said.

∽

The next day I started my new job. I huddled into my coat as I battled through a stream of people rushing to work. The weather fit my mood—heartsick, weary and weighted down by the pressure of fitting into a new corporate role. I had been surprised when they hired me because the interviews didn't go well and I didn't hear back for weeks. I was probably not their first choice but I was here now as an Executive Assistant to some big wigs at a legal media company near Wall Street.

I was grateful to be out of retail but also thinking, *how the hell am I going to keep it together at a desk, for eight hours, in a corporate office?* It was the middle of December, freezing outside with no sun in sight and not likely for at least five more months. There must have been Christmas celebrations going on somewhere, but I didn't see the twinkling lights or festive decorations. I could only see the morose clouds hanging low in the sky and feel the winter wind whipping down the avenues.

I sat on the train with thousands of others all dressed the same, clutching laptop bags and handbags close to their chests, the women in runners with impractical high heels in the shopping bags at their feet. *Who was I kidding?* I didn't belong with the suits, wearing my skull rain boots and a feather clip in my hair, unstoppable tears still leaking down my cheeks.

That first week, I cried the entire way to and from work on the subway. I wore dark sunglasses in an effort to hide, though it was pretty obvious to anyone with eyes. Every lunch break I called my mom and then would go have another quiet cry in the bathroom stalls. I was smoking close to a pack of cigarettes a day, all the while my mom suffered from lung cancer.

Every day after work, I picked up two bottles of red Italian wine on the way home and spent the rest of the night crying and drinking in our teeny kitchen with Amanda and Bella. I wanted to get over it and move on from Finn, but at the end of the day, I still wanted to be with him.

~

Amanda and I decided we needed a break. We needed warmth and sunshine. We needed to dance and laugh. When daylight still hadn't managed to break the December gloom, we took the plunge and booked tickets to Costa Rica.

I called Finn to let him know that I was going away.

"Sounds awesome. You'll have a great time," Finn said. He only spoke in careful, measured tones to me now. The new Finn wasn't as open and didn't try to go deep with me. I was hoping things would repair themselves with time. Time would heal this wound. *Isn't that how it works?*

I didn't want to leave things like this though. I sighed and took a deep breath. "We need to talk about us, Finn. We can't just keep going on like this. I want things to get better."

Finn was quiet for a moment. On the Skype call, I could see that he was looking out the window.

"Let's just talk when you get back, OK?" he said, turning back to the monitor. "Have a good trip." Then he was gone.

It took me still another few weeks to realize that he was really, truly gone. This is how delusional young love can be.

∽

We were back from Costa Rica and amongst the familiar cold of New York City. "I'm just going to get online quickly," I called out to Amanda. We'd just walked into the apartment from the airport after stopping to pick up Bella from the dog sitter. We were all happy to be home, but Bella was the happiest. She was tearing back and forth across the entire apartment, jumping between my bed and Amanda's – rolling around on the ground, thrilled to pieces just to be back together.

Amanda laughed, "You're such a goof, Bella!" She looked up at me. "Finn?" she asked. She didn't need to say more.

Costa Rica had been everything that we needed it to be. Warm, sunny, raw. A place where Christmas and the New Year could pass in a haze of Imperial beer on the beach in the afternoons, and Cacique Guaro Rum cocktails at the beach bars in the evenings.

I'd hoped the time away would help me recover from the dark times and miserable feelings. But Finn had never really left my mind. I was cut off from social media, from calls and texts, and while that had been the case, I felt like my old self. I could keep the obsessing at bay. But as soon as I was back on "land", I was desperate to see what he was doing.

I flopped down on the bed and grabbed my laptop. It hadn't been turned on in weeks, but it powered straight up. *I'll just check Facebook quickly.* I typed in Finn's name, my heart beating fast and my hands shaking. It took me a couple of tries to get the spelling of his name right.

I held my breath, which I expelled in a short, sharp burst when his profile popped up. It only took a moment of scrolling to see that he'd been to a music festival over the New Year holiday. Then I saw what I'd been dreading. He hadn't been alone. There, for the whole world to see, were smiling, "couple-y" pictures of him with another girl – Sarah. I knew, *knew* that this is the girl he had cheated with. I felt bile rise in my throat. They already looked in love.

I shut down the computer and slumped back onto the bed. In my soul, I'd known it was over before I left for Costa Rica, but I didn't want to believe it. I felt myself begin a downward spiral. The tears flowed. I felt ashamed because I still cared so much. I was afraid that I might never find a love like Finn again and I felt bitterly sad, knowing something I had cared so much about was gone.

How could he move on so fast? How could he be so happy while I'm so completely miserable? She's so pretty. Were we in the SAME relationship? It doesn't make sense. Did I mean anything to him? I wonder what she's like? She's probably amazing. Was he lying? Was I lying to myself? Is my intuition off? How could I have been so wrong?

We set up a skype call a few days later to officially end the relationship.

"I love you, but I'm not *in* love with you," he said.

I wanted to scream at that overused and insincere tagline. That's not love! When you love someone, you try to make it work. You support them when their mom gets sick. You make moves and effort to be together.

Finally, my sadness was replaced by anger – good, fresh, cleansing anger. I was furious. Steaming. But not at Finn…at myself. I had known for a while that he didn't love me the way I wanted to feel loved but I hadn't accepted it. So, I betrayed my feelings because I wouldn't let it go.

I hung up the phone. I was angry but it was a relief. Anger I could handle. Anger was the beginning of my transformation.

Chapter 6

COMBUSTION

It was not only Fat Tuesday, otherwise known as Mardi Gras (in French), but it was also my birthday. 25. A quarter-century. My mom was sick. I was sad, ashamed and scared that I might never be able to make things right with her. I worried that I could never forgive her for everything I believed she'd done– to me, to my siblings and especially to my dad. I felt regret for the disrespect I'd heaped on her over the years.

A couple of weeks before, Amanda and I agreed that the only place to be on Fat Tuesday was the Mardi Gras epicenter, New Orleans. The streets were lit by neon lights and music throbs from every corner. The balconies were hung with strands of multi-colored beads, flashing in the light, and nearly as many people, in as many colors. It was riotous, sensory and wonderful.

We spent the first night on Bourbon Street with our friends Miguel and Lawrence. It was jammed with people, from one side of the street to the other – young and old – all clutching foot-long blended drinks or Pat O'Brien's famous Hurricanes, orange

Rum cocktails. The flashing lights and partying on Bourbon Street soon wore us out, so we decided to see a jazz band on our last night in "Nolens" instead.

Before heading out, we mixed the cheapest vodka we could find with Red Bull, Watermelon Four Lokos (an alcoholic energy drink banned in most states) and a splash of champagne, just to keep it classy. Lawrence and Miguel serenaded us out the door and through the French Quarter. The fretwork balconies, pastel-colored townhouses and voodoo shops were so quintessentially New Orleans, but by this stage, we barely noticed. Maybe due to the Four Lokos.

The Jazz bar was intimate, with only seven or eight tables for four people. We arrived early and sat down at our table to order a drink. The table was sticky under my forearms, and the venue felt hot and overcrowded, even though it was nothing like Bourbon Street. We all ordered drinks – now we were on the whiskeys. It was going to be a fun night.

I excused myself to go to the bathroom and headed across the room to the ladies. The whiskey warmed me and I felt like I was floating. I pushed open the black stall door and sat down on the toilet and the tears began to fall. I was shocked, caught by surprise. I wasn't just crying but bawling, unable to catch my breath.

Every time I gasped for air, I felt simultaneously the hope that it would be over soon and the absolute overwhelming belief that it would never end. Terrible darkness was coming from deep within me, it was part of me yet I was powerless. I couldn't regain control; I had no choice but to give in. I didn't know it then but I was having a panic attack.

Amanda came down to check on me. When I saw her, my sadness finally took shape.

"I didn't think I would be here at 25 years old. I didn't think this would be my life," I said. Then I heard myself say this repeatedly while sobbing as Amanda stroked my back and wiped my tears away.

While Mom and our issues laid heavily on my mind, genuinely, at the time, I believed this fear and sadness were mainly related to Finn. I thought I'd lost irreplaceable love.

Amanda stayed with me and through my tears, I heard her speaking, telling me how amazing I was, how much my friends and family loved me and how much I'd grown. Lawrence came to the door at some point. He couldn't go in and I could barely acknowledge him, but I heard Amanda telling him it was OK, she got it.

Amanda came back and knelt beside me. I still hadn't stopped crying.

"Go back to the boys," I finally said. "Go back. I'll be OK." I don't know if it was true but I felt an overwhelming need to be alone.

"No way. I'm not leaving," she said.

"You're missing the whole show," I said between sobs.

"So what," she said. "It's just Jazz."

"It's ok, go. I need a bit of space," I said. She didn't want to go, but finally, she let me convince her. She left me be. I stayed on the floor, still crying until I heard the band finishing. I knew then that I had to do something. I had to get out of that bathroom, or I never would.

I slowed my breathing, taking deeper breaths through my nose and exhaling longer out of my mouth. In and out, in and out. This will pass, I told myself. It always does. Finally, after what seemed hours, I pulled myself out of the stall. I coached myself to the sink where I splashed water on my face, still breathing in and out, slowing my breath. Then I coached myself out the door and sat at the table as if nothing had happened. I had missed the entire show.

I didn't want to talk about what had happened or why. I felt shame stacking onto deeper shame. Amanda stayed close for the rest of the night and we still managed to get out and party. Enough so that we all ended up missing our early morning flights home the next day.

Nothing really changed after what happened in that bathroom. It wouldn't be my last panic attack.

I spent the next two and a half years *knowing* my lifestyle was unsustainable and it was making me sick. I knew something was wrong but was unwilling (or maybe unable) to change. To rip apart the patterns so new patterns could form. I told myself that this was just my quarter-life crisis – that it happened to everyone – and I hung my hat on that fact. I didn't need to make any changes then. I was happy riding the tidal waves.

∼

After my mom's first round of chemo, she was assigned a new doctor. The new doctor quickly recognized that she'd been misdiagnosed. He ordered more scans and found a tumor the size of a softball on her ovaries. This explained the cancer cells they found in her lungs. New diagnosis - stage four ovarian cancer. Prognosis- chemotherapy, surgery and more chemo. While this was the worst stage of cancer, mom was a fighter and was never going to give up.

Mom was taking chemo like a champ. Her hair fell out but she fully embraced the bald head. She even still had an appetite. She continued to visit New Jersey whenever she could and she'd always make sure to get her favorite pizza, bagels and Taylor Ham. She was in great spirits, making jokes and travelling, working and going about life as usual.

She kept making plans. She'd talk about her next trip to Florida to see my sister and wanted to plan a trip with me to visit the Caribbean. She didn't seem to worry that she might not be around. She didn't acknowledge it at all. She didn't let the chemo slow her down in the slightest. She never let anybody see her sweat. That was my mom, Carol-Ann.

That April she went in for surgery to remove the tumor. The operation was complex, especially considering her body was vulnerable after months of chemotherapy and with a weakened immune system she'd be extra susceptible to infection. I sat in the hospital in West Virginia with Eddie, my mom's partner, my Aunt Millie and Aunt Rose waiting for good news. This time we avoided the hospital coffee and took turns ducking out to a nearby coffee shop to keep caffeinated.

Eddie and my mom had been together for seven years at this stage, but my dad and mom had never divorced. They'd never even separated officially. I never really understood what kept them "together" yet apart. There was love between them; my dad brought a sense of safety to my mom's life. But in every other way, she was with Eddie.

Except when she came to New Jersey. Then for all intents and purposes, it was like they were still in a marriage. They slept in the same room, made jokes and cared for us kids. When she was in Jersey, their relationship was like any traditional marriage; only there was nothing traditional about it.

When the surgeon came into the room to talk to all of us, including my mom, I could tell from the way his eyes shifted when he spoke that it wasn't good news. There was more than one tumor and they couldn't get them all. So, they lasered what was left and would take a "wait and see approach." That is when I saw my mom as a vulnerable scared little girl. The look in her eyes was more heartbreaking than how the stitches down her entire front torso looked. I knew they were hoping for the best. We all were.

They never told us a specific timeline, but we all knew what stage four cancer meant. A few days, a few weeks, a few months or a few years if were fortunate. My mom continued with chemo and took it day by day, the only thing she could do. We all did the same.

∼

That summer in New York City the streets were hot, viscerally hot, the asphalt soft underfoot, the buildings and streets shimmering like a mirage. In Chinatown, the stench of humanity and accumulating garbage hit you in the face like a living thing. If I think about it, I can still smell that stench stuck in the back of my throat. There's nothing else like it in the world. Unlike most people, I don't mind the hot, humid, sticky summers in New York; it's my favorite season.

I had multiple Australian friends visiting at various times that summer. We would pile out the door into the dark city nights, heading to the cool new restaurants or the amplified heat of crowded dive bars.

Our nights followed a pattern: A delicious restaurant, often in Brooklyn or one of the villages, so we could try the newest thing – whether it was an oyster bar, authentic Italian or Mexican sushi fusion. Then we'd hit up rooftop bars, locals or New York City's best dive bars, where we'd drink and inevitably end up dancing (regardless of whether there was a dance floor or not) - getting lost in the music and the vibrations in our own little world. We'd brush sweaty skin against sweaty skin as we drank bottles of beer, champagne and trays of pickleback shots to chase the heat. We capped the summer off with a trip to Ibiza where we danced away our worries; ecstasy in every form.

When we arrived back on American shores, tanner than ever, our lease was up, so I decided to move to New Jersey with my dad, to my childhood home. I didn't want to leave Amanda or the city, but I also didn't want to be locked into a lease when my mom's health could rapidly decline.

Living in New Jersey didn't affect my existence. I kept doing what I did best – travelling at the drop of a hat and exploring as many things as I possibly could…burning both ends of the candle. I gathered up my experiences like a collector, believing each one was more important than the last. I took every opportunity that I could to try something, feel something, and live. I wanted to live like my mom had every day of her life.

Age 10

Chapter 7

BURNING INDEX

The year that I was 10, my mom turned my family's world upside down.

"It's hot," I complained, rolling over on the family room carpet where I was lying, watching television with my younger sister, Cassy. "There's nothing to do." Cassy didn't reply, she just kept her brown eyes focused on the screen. My dad was in his chair with the newspaper open, but he didn't seem to be reading much.

"Uggh," I moaned. It was August. A few weeks until school started and I was in absolute despair because we were moving. My mom was packing my sister, my two brothers and me up and moving us to West Virginia. West Virginia! All my friends were in New Jersey. My school was there. But she didn't care.

I heard the distinctive sound of a car pulling up on the street in front of our house and my heart sank.

I popped onto the couch and pulled aside the long white curtains, peering through the window and into the heat of the day. A red van was pulled up outside the house. As I watched, the hazard lights came on and a man stepped out of the car.

He hitched up his pants. He was a big guy – 6'3" and 300 pounds at least. He smiled, his dentures gleaming, as my mom walked out to the curb. She had Sadie, our Weimaraner on her leash and a cardboard box under one arm. When she handed the box to the man, I knew he must be Jack, the man who was moving with us to West Virginia. I heard his name whispered and the voice I heard on the phone asking for my mom.

Jack pulled open the van's back doors and slid the box inside. Then he took Sadie's lead and urged her into the van's side door. I looked over at my dad. He was staring resolutely at his paper, but his hand reached out and grasped mine, giving it a little squeeze.

Two hours later Jack, my mom, Cassy, Rob, Rick and I were crammed in the red van on our way to West Virginia. I cried the entire way down with my pillowcase "twiddle" over my face sitting in the back next to our cockatiel bird, Charlie. Sadie was in the middle between mom and Jack. Every so often she gave a little whimper. Halfway there she got car sick. I knew just how she felt.

"I hate you. I hate you!" I whispered into the folds of my tear-soaked twiddle, as we left everything that I knew behind.

∼

My mom always did what she wanted to do, no matter what. Moving my brothers, sister and me to a three-bedroom trailer on a dirt road in West Virginia with a truck driver called Jack was just the pinnacle of her behavior. She said she moved us because our neighborhood was getting dangerous and all of us kids were falling in with the wrong crowd. That may have been true. My brother Rob was skipping school and getting brought home by the cops. Rick, my other brother was smoking weed and I was smoking cigarettes, whenever we could sneak them from our parents. It was probably part of her decision to protect us from these unsavory elements, but at the end of the day, she moved us to West Virginia because she wanted to. Regardless of how it made me, my siblings and especially my dad feel.

I was so angry with her at the time and carried that resentment throughout my life. Even when things were good between us, I never could let it go. How could she be so selfish? How could she do this to Dad?

But at the same time, she was my mom, I loved her. I admired how she embraced life. When she saw what she wanted, she went after it, no matter what. She was willing to make hard decisions and difficult changes to find her happiness. She didn't give a fuck what other people thought. Or at least that is certainly how it seemed to me.

It took me some time to realize the truth and when I did it hit me full force: I was just like her.

∼

During my time in New York, I lived for no one but myself. I embraced life, often to disastrous or hilarious consequences with a sprinkling of Sex and the City moments. There was the waiter from brunch who turned out to have a micropenis, and the 6'4" Norwegian, with a man bun whom I called Thor because I never learned his real name. I accidentally left an ex's phone number on his table instead of mine. Whoops! No wonder he never called.

One evening, sneaking up a staircase in a building neither one of us lived in to have some fun on the rooftop, and another evening, when the opportunity presented itself, letting loose on a famous director's yacht.

But eventually, your stories start creating patterns that are impossible to ignore. I was chasing highs, using alcohol to escape, distract or numb and mismanaging my energy. When I would attract a nice guy, I would quickly grow bored, finding a reason to put them off. But the *other* guys, the guys that flirted heavily and were happy to hook up after a night of drinking but then wouldn't call for weeks. You know, the ones who were unavailable physically, mentally or emotionally…those were the guys I found myself being pulled toward. Like attracts like, I guess?

I also noticed as my mom's health started to decline, the game grew old. One night, I was riding home on the subway with my evening date when suddenly he stood up at a random stop and got off the train without saying a single word to me, without acknowledging I was even there. The next day he texted me, "Hey." One word.

What was I doing? Why was I chasing after assholes who would leave me alone on a train at night sending one-word text messages to check in with me!? Next thing you know, I'll be getting dumped by a post-it note!

∼

From what I understand, Jack wasn't the first time my mom cheated on my dad, but it was the first time that she left him.

I can't recall much of my childhood, but the story goes that my mom started hanging out with a family friend named Jerry before I was born. She was drinking heavily on the weekends. Jerry was a drinking buddy who turned into more.

What I remember about Jerry comes in snapshots – dark hair, smeared glasses, thick arms covered in a sheen of rough hair. I can still picture his tiny one-bedroom basement floor apartment, with no kitchen, across the street from the park. He had a red light in his bathroom and an old popcorn tin full of candy called the "candy can". Whenever he saw me, he'd always sing my name like a song, "Ka ka ka kaaaaaty, she's a lady." I remember feeling creeped out before I even knew what being creeped out meant.

During the summer holidays, we'd see Jerry at the beach. My mom would take us down there on the long hot afternoons, and they'd split a beer while my brother and I splashed in the freezing New Jersey surf. My dad was never there of course, but he knew. He was always working and hated the beach. But my mom loved the beach and it must have been appealing to spend time with someone else who did.

The year I turned five and started kindergarten, everything changed. Jerry wasn't around anymore. My mom gave up drinking and Cassy was born. My mom started walking me and my brother Rick to school every day, pushing Cassy in her little blue stroller. She also started volunteering in class, reading to us at night and packing us lunches with pizza Lunchables – just like the other kids.

My older two siblings had a different version of Mom when they were my age. They had walked themselves to school and Dee, the eldest, had to be a mom to all of us. It was different for her and Rob.

I was too young to remember my mom like that. My

childhood seemed just like everyone else's and I always felt close to my mom. I was her little princess. Of course, the only thing in life you can count on is that things change.

Age 4

Chapter 8

FLAMMABLE

My mom and dad were neighbors growing up in Harrison, New Jersey. My dad claims he was in love with my mom since the day they met, but he couldn't convince her to go out with him until she was sixteen and he was nineteen. After that, it was a done deal. It wasn't a unique story, either. My mom's brother and my dad's sister married and had a baby, so my cousin Paul is related from both sides.

They say opposites attract, and that was certainly the case with my parents. Dad had a 1968 black Chevy Camaro with tombstones painted down the side and was voted "Most Shy" in high school. My mom didn't drive until she was forty-two years old and was a free spirit. My mom's father was an alcoholic who couldn't keep a job, so my grandmother did the best she could to raise nine children on her own, while on welfare. On the other hand, my dad grew up with strict Polish parents and just a small tight-knit family with only two siblings. One thing they did have in common was humble beginnings.

After dating in their teenage years, they had my sister, Dee, fairly young, but didn't marry until my mom was in her mid-twenties when Rob came along. I think they were probably happy once, in those early days. But it didn't seem to stick. My older siblings talked about my mom in the days before I was born, or at least before I can remember. They paint a picture of a woman who was always going out with friends, who would come home smashed on the weekends or not at all.

They described a woman I didn't recognize, not until I took a hard look in the mirror when I was in my twenties to find her looking back at me.

∼

I distinctly remember Jack's thick southern accent on the other end of the phone line. "Is Kaaaaayyyy-rooll theeeyyyrrrreee." He talked slowly, just like some of my cousins from West Virginia. Plus, we had a caller ID. I was a curious kid who needed to know what this man and my mom chatted about every night.

In those days, there was a trick to picking up the phone without anybody noticing. I'd seen my older sister do it, so I tried a few times with our early 80s cabbage patch phone. The phone was an actual cabbage patch girl in a pink dress, with long blonde hair and a big pink bow just above each ear. She wore white sneakers with white socks and the beige receiver hung on her right forearm. If you did it correctly, you *could* listen in on conversations by quickly getting your finger on the lever while covering the bottom end of the phone simultaneously. Most of the time my mom would hear the click on the line and yell, "Kate, get off the phone!" She'd always had a sixth sense.

Those times I did manage to listen in, she spoke quietly and didn't seem to hide anything. A few times she crawled into my bed late at night while still on the cordless phone talking to Jack. She must have thought I was asleep. Did she want me to listen? Was this her way of letting me know what was going on? How could she do this to my dad? How could my dad allow it? It was a strange feeling to want to have adult conversations with my mother that I knew I would never have. I felt powerless and frustrated.

I would have traded any American Girl doll outfit for someone to explain why there were so many secrets. Of course, there were many other secrets that I would find out eventually, starting with Rob.

~

My brother Rob was fifteen when he discovered the truth about his biological parents. There were times when I felt Rob was different. He had unique traits the rest of us lacked. Where our faces were slim and angular, his was round and soft. He had dark thick hair, especially on his chest. Rob was open and emotional whereas everyone else was always determined not to show they cared. But I was ten years old when I first realized Rob *was* different.

My dad and mom were arguing again. There had been more late-night phone calls than usual, and my mom was distracted. She had that look in her eye too, that secret, inward look.

My parents were in their bedroom. I knew they were arguing from the urgent back and forth of their voices. But suddenly my dad's voice rang loudly through the house. 'Why don't you send

Rob down to his real father then?' I heard him say. Then the door immediately slammed shut. There was nothing more to hear, but what else did we need to hear?

Dee had pieced together bits of conversation over the years and already believed Rob was adopted. Besides overhearing a lot of things from my parents and extended family, she had always felt that Rob was treated *differently* but never said anything to him. She hadn't felt it was her place. He had to find out on his own.

You would think the natural step would be to approach my parents about it first, but we didn't speak to our parents directly. It just wasn't how our family communicated. So, Rob tried to figure it out himself. He started digging through family photo albums and papers. He didn't know what he was looking for, he just felt the need to look.

Growing up, my parents talked about my grandmother on my mom's side having nine kids. However, when our family got together there was only my mom, three aunts and four uncles. I wasn't great at math, but I knew that was only eight. Nobody mentioned the missing sibling, we knew something wasn't right, we just didn't know this had anything to do with Rob.

One day, Rob and his friend Victor were flipping through family photo albums when Victor pointed to a woman.

"Who's that?" Victor asked.

"Ah, that's my Aunt Rose," he said. But as Robbie pulled the album toward him, he dropped an old newspaper clipping. The boys picked it up, unfolding it carefully. Perhaps they already knew that what it contained was important. The headline said, "Mother's Day Massacre" and the article read, "Kathy Skidlo leaves behind husband Jack Skidlo and fifteen-month-old son, Robert James."

Robert James is Rob's name.

Rob's birth mom was my Aunt Kathy, my mom's younger sister. She'd been shot on Mother's Day when Rob was only fifteen months old. The family never got any answers other than the convicted person claimed insanity and only served five years in jail, then was free to walk the streets of New Jersey again. My grandmother lost a daughter. My mom lost a sister. Rob lost a mother and Jack lost a wife but they never spoke of her again. It was like they just wiped her from the family line. As I said, direct communication didn't run in my family.

Rob wasn't my brother, but my first cousin, yet he will always be our brother, no matter what. My parents hid this fact from all of us for 15 years. More mysteriously, they didn't tell Rob. Perhaps a sign of the era where emotional honesty was not as valued as it is today.

Everyone knew Jack wasn't Rob's biological father yet nobody knew who was and still doesn't to this day. For my mom, blood is thicker than water; in her eyes, Rob was blood, and Jack was not. My grandmother couldn't possibly take on a tenth child so my parents married. They went down to Town Hall because they were about to take Jack to court for custody over Rob and the court required my parents to be married to approve the adoption. There were no bells and whistles. No fancy wedding ceremony.

At the tender age of 25 and 28, they found themselves married with two kids. Maybe it wasn't the best way to start a marriage, and I'm not clear how involved my dad was in the decision-making or if he was just brought along for the ride, but certainly, he would have done anything for my mom. And that never changed for him as long as she was alive.

My uncle took Rob to Kathy's gravesite and explained what had happened with his mom. When Rob finally found the courage to talk to my mom about what he'd found out, she was in the basement doing laundry. He walked into the basement and sat on the bottom stair. He looked over at my mom, standing next to the dryer, with the phone in one hand and sorting through laundry with the other.

"Ma, can you please get off the phone? There's something I need to talk to you about," Rob said.

My mom said, "What, Rob? What do you want?"

"Ma, get off the phone, I need to talk to you about something. NOW. It's important." Rob's face was pale and his voice was rising with determination to finally get the truth out in the open.

My mom realized Rob's seriousness was so she turned to her standby, deflecting with humor. "Ah what now Rob, did you get some girl pregnant or something?"

Rob, increasingly frustrated, said, "What? NO! Jesus mom, can you please just get off the phone?"

"All right, fine," she said. "Hey, can I call you back?" She clicked off the cordless but kept it in her hand and continued gazing down at the unsorted laundry.

"I know about my real mom."

My mom paused for a split second but didn't look up. She threw some stuff in the dryer and slammed the door shut. Leaning back on her heels she said, "Well good, now you know." Rob responded in disbelief, "Is that it? I was expecting a conversation, like were you ever planning to tell me?"

"Kathy was involved with some bad people. It messed her up," my mom said. Then she grabbed the laundry basket and walked up the basement stairs past Rob. And that was that. Nothing more was ever discussed. No more information or explanation was ever given to him. It was just another secret shame that he, and the rest of us, had to carry on our shoulders.

Curious and confused were common feelings in our house, but I was often too uncomfortable or scared to say anything. Rob was brave that day when he confronted my mom. Unfortunately, he didn't get what he needed. He didn't get a sense of comfort, security or emotional safety.

To this day, my parents have never discussed Rob's adoption or his birth parents with us. I once asked dad why they never told us. He said, "We just assumed you'd all eventually find out anyway."

∼

They also say it comes in threes. When I was ten, I found out Rob was not our biological brother, we moved to West Virginia leaving behind everything that I knew and that year, I was also molested in our cubby house. It was a year of change, upheaval, worry, uncertainty and endless secrets.

Mom was right, West Virginia would prove to be a blessing in a lot of ways. It distanced us from some of the bad influences in our lives that were part and parcel of the New Jersey lifestyle. But it was hard to see that during the eight-hour car ride from New Jersey to West Virginia.

I left my six-bedroom, family home five miles outside of New York City and arrived via dirt, pothole-scarred road to a tiny three-bedroom trailer in Bumblefuck, Nowhere. At the time I couldn't believe what was happening. How could my mom do this to us?

My mom never hid that I was her "favorite," so I got to share the master bedroom with her. It had two closets, a queen-size waterbed, an ensuite and a separate Jacuzzi bath. My brothers had to share a room only big enough to fit two twin-size beds and my little sister had a playroom in the back. She slept on the couch though because she was deathly afraid of her dolls after watching the movie, "Child's Play," starring the murderous doll "Chucky."

Our water came from a covered well in the yard. It was filled with iron so you couldn't drink it and it smelled like rotten eggs from Sulphur. It eventually started turning my blonde hair orange, so I stopped washing my hair with it. I can still see my mom walking off down the dirt road, with Sadie behind her, an empty gallon milk jug in each hand to a natural spring, where she'd fill up the jugs and trudge them back home for clean drinking water. She performed this ritual every morning until we realized we could fill them up at the laundromat in town, something we weren't meant to be doing, or when we went to my Aunt Rose's house, two hours away.

The land, the trailer, and the smelly water – these were Jack's, the man who had picked us up in his red van and moved us to West Virginia. He earned his living as a trucker and was on the road a lot, a fact I was grateful for. We had more space when he was away. Because he wasn't home a lot, I didn't have that much to do with him. But I remember coming home from school one day and hearing Jack and my mom having sex. I was horrified. I couldn't understand what she was doing with him, that she'd leave my dad, our big home in New Jersey and tear apart our family for a trucker with a big belly and three-bedroom trailer.

I didn't believe she loved him. She seemed to be using him, but it was hard to understand why or for what. It didn't feel like she'd somehow given us a better life, and it certainly didn't feel like a trade-up. Even through all my pre-teen anger, I felt bad for Jack sometimes. He was a decent guy, who treated us kids well and was nice to my mom. He was kind, always trying to tell jokes and bought us things when needed. But my mom treated him just like she had my dad. Hot then cold with an attitude of "take it or leave it." When my mom wanted something enough, she didn't veer off her path for anybody. She had incredible vision and focus. And she wanted us in West Virginia.

∼

It had been a few weeks since we'd been uprooted and moved to West Virginia. Cassy was playing with sticks in the dirt, already a proper hillbilly. She wore white cowboy boots with my sparkly peach dancing school leotard, grubby from weeks of wear. I watched her, bored. I hadn't made any friends yet.

So, I decided to rummage through my mom's closet to see what I could steal to wear the next day. I was hoping to find something new, but all that was buried in her closet were black and grey Harley Davidson t-shirts. As far as I knew, she'd never been on a Harley, yet they were the *only* shirts she wore. She was fashionably ahead of her time and although I didn't think they were cool then, I cherish these same shirts now.

I was about to shut the closet doors when my foot kicked something on the ground buried under the clothes. It was an old blue Adidas shoebox. Curious I slid it toward me, hoping to find a pair of sandals or new sneakers I could "borrow". But when I opened it, I sighed in disappointment.

The box was filled with odds and ends, old receipts, a silver lighter, concert ticket stubs and my Aunt Kathy's death certificate.

When I looked at the certificate, I saw Robert James under the Surviving Child section. Only then did I realize who Rob's real mom was for the first time. This was my proof that my parents weren't Rob's parents. Not only that but I saw that my Aunt Kathy was married when she died. In the box next to Surviving Spouse it said, Jack Skidlo. My stomach dropped. That was the name from the caller-ID.

Could this be the same Jack Skidlo whose home I sat in now? The Jack that my mom was having sex with, that she'd moved us here to West Virginia to be with – could this be her dead sister's husband?

"What the hell," I whispered under my breath. I was emboldened by the sound of my voice. "Oh my God, so gross," I said louder. Her dead sister's husband. Could this be any more disgusting? Rob already knew, but I wasn't aware of the details before this moment.

I stood up quickly and shoved the closet doors shut, burying the offending papers. The doors caught on the runners and jammed – they always did if you didn't slide them closed just so.

"Ugh!" I kicked the doors for good measure and left them half open. Almost hiding her secrets. Almost, but not quite.

∼

It wasn't worth it. Approaching my mom with personal questions made her defensive and she'd start yelling in no time. So, I pretended the information didn't exist and carried on as a ten-year-old does. I didn't say anything to my siblings either about what I'd found. And I sure as hell was not telling my friends at school. They'd sign me up for the Jerry Springer show if word got out. Sadly, this pattern of silence and secrets would mean I would miss the chance with my mom to clear the air and get answers to these questions.

A few weeks after these discoveries, I ran into my room, heart thumping, and tossed my bag down on the bed where it missed the dark green bedspread. I didn't care. I spun around in a circle – I was so excited – I was going to Chloe's house for a sleepover. My first sleepover ever!

Three other girls were invited, so we were going to dress up like the Spice Girls and I was to be Baby Spice – Chloe decided this only made sense because of my blonde hair. It made sense to me too – she was my favorite Spice Girl. Now all I needed was to find just the right outfit. I started rummaging through the wooden drawers built into the frame of the waterbed where most of my clothes were kept.

My mom walked into our bedroom. She straightened the bedspread before sitting down on the edge of the bed. She crossed her legs and then her ankles. As usual, she was wearing jeans and a Harley Davidson t-shirt. For a moment she just watched me tossing aside various outfit possibilities, not one of them right for Baby Spice.

Then she spoke. "Kate, how would you feel about a baby brother or sister?"

My entire body froze, my right hand still clutching the perfect pink plaid miniskirt. I quickly realized what that meant – this was not a baby with my father, but with Jack. This stranger. This man should be my *uncle*, not the father of my little brother or sister. My face flushed hot and I felt like I was choking.

Somehow, I managed to speak, letting out each word slowly for fear if I rushed, I wouldn't be clear. "If you have a baby, I will hate it and you for the rest of my life. I won't hold it, talk to it or even consider it one of my siblings," I said.

"Kate, you don't mean? That's pretty harsh. C'mon."

"Yes, I mean it, I swear. I will hate you and the baby for the rest of my life. You're disgusting. I can't believe you." I was now out of control, crying and on the verge of hysterical.

"C'mon Kate, I can't help what has already happened."

"Well, you should have thought about that before! No! I will NEVER be okay with this. Leave me alone. Get out. I don't want to talk to you anymore, ever again." I grabbed her hand and pulled her toward the door.

She left the room, shutting the door quietly behind her, which was almost worse than her slamming it. I continued to cry for a couple of minutes, but I had to pull myself together because we were about to leave for Chloe's house and I didn't want to be late.

I pulled on a cobbled-together Baby Spice outfit and put my hair into side ponytails. My eyes were red and my skin was blotchy. All her fault.

I was completely silent during the entire 30-minute car ride, and when we finally pulled up outside Chloe's large, solid brick home, the kind of home I wish we had, I was already opening the car door. I jumped out as soon as the car stopped, slamming the door shut and cutting off my mom's goodbyes. I walked away without looking back.

The following day, I called my mom to see what time she could come to pick me up. I was still pissed at her, so I talked as little as possible.

"What time are you coming to get me?" I asked.

"I'll be there around 3, is that okay honey?"

HONEY!? Don't act like nothing's wrong! However, I couldn't shout at her in the middle of Chloe's living room, so I said nothing.

She could sense I wasn't going to speak so she continued. "Don't worry honey, I peed on the stick wrong. I'm not having a baby."

I didn't know what to say to that, so I just said, "Uh-huh, k bye." I hung up the phone and walked back into the kitchen where Chloe's mom was making pancakes and her dad was setting the table. I settled on my chair and looked around. On the inside, I was a raging cauldron of chaos while I sat in a scene of contented domestic bliss.

My mom had been pregnant of course, but had an abortion, behind Jack's back or against his wishes and he was understandably upset. Was it my fault? I didn't know the details then, but I knew something had happened between mom and Jack because we had all moved out before long.

We moved in with Meg, Dan and their two kids, family friends from way back. They lived "up a crick" and were as West Virginian as you could find with hearts of gold. One of my strongest memories was of Dan standing in the twilight, catching a bat that had flown in the front door with his bare hands. He didn't even flinch.

Soon after my mom found out she was pregnant; she called my dad and told him the situation. She cried on the phone, expressing that she didn't want to have any child but his. My dad sensed the depth of his kids' vulnerability, took out a second mortgage on our house in New Jersey and bought Jack's trailer and land so we could move back in. Needless to say, Jack wasn't part of the deal, but my dad didn't move in with us either.

My mom and dad had an estranged relationship for the next five or so years. They didn't date other people and were still legally married, even though they lived separately in different states. They talked all the time and my dad continued to pay for the things we needed and wanted.

Every school break for Thanksgiving, Christmas, Easter and summer my mom would drive me, Rick and Cassy up to New Jersey to spend the holidays with dad. Rob joined the military and Dee was finishing college. My dad worked as a mechanic for 12 hours a day so we barely saw him, but we still went every school break. My mom would stay with us as well, and while we were there, she would act like we were one big normal family. She would even sleep in my dad's bed.

Nobody questioned my mother and you wouldn't want to. It was still her home, her bedroom, her children, so what? She lived life on her terms. That was my mom. We realized from a young age what we could and could not control, and fighting against what we couldn't control got us nowhere…real fast!

Faja & Mamacita

Family Photo

Family Photo

High School Graduation

Chapter 9

FIRE TRIANGLE

In my last year of high school, Dad came to West Virginia to look into buying a new home for us all to live in together. I remember walking through a beautiful log cabin home, the sunlight streaming off the polished floor and my dad and mom together as if they'd never been apart. I was dreaming of which bedroom would be mine. Nothing had been said out loud, but I assumed it meant my parents were getting back together. I shouldn't have assumed anything.

Just when it looked like things were going well for my parents, my mom started getting those phone calls again – this time from some guy called Eddie. It was a Jersey number, so naturally, I was curious. Who was this guy? Did we know him?

By now, I wasn't a little girl anymore. I knew what this meant. I could only assume my mother was having another relationship. Even while the phone calls increased my mom and dad were looking for houses together. I kept my mouth shut and anticipated another man in our lives.

∽

It was Easter break and we were all up in New Jersey to see my dad again, though my mom had been staying out more than usual. I had just brushed my teeth and went in to give my dad his goodnight kiss. I never missed that ritual. Dad was standing next to his bed, just about to turn the fan and television on, so I stood on my tiptoes to kiss his cheek. "Goodnight Faja. Love you," I said.

I turned to head out but just before I got to the door my dad said, "Kate, what's going on with Mommy? She's not answering my calls or getting back to me about stuff. I thought I was going to move to West Virginia with you guys, but I don't know what the hell is going on?"

My heart broke. He sounded so small and sad. I'd hoped maybe she'd told him what was going on, but of course, she hadn't. She'd just gone on doing what she liked without a worry about anyone else's feelings.

Feeling like I was going to vomit and cry at the same time, I said, "Dad, I don't know what's going on but I see a number from New Jersey on the caller ID a lot. He's calling for Mommy. I think his name is Eddie?" I shrugged. "I don't know."

My dad's shoulders slumped, and he sat down on the edge of the bed. He nodded slightly and then tried to smile at me.

Now I felt rage. My mom was a coward. I didn't want to be forced to keep her secrets. I shouldn't have to deliver the bad news. They were the grown-ups, not me.

Of all my mom's games and betrayals, my dad seemed to take this one the hardest. It was only a short time after that he came to my high school graduation in West Virginia drastically thinner. I knew it wasn't from diet and exercise because he didn't look happier.

When school was out for the summer, that meant our usual three-month stay in New Jersey with Dad; my mom also came for a few weeks. She was still sleeping in his bed and coming and going, all while continuing to date Eddie.

One morning I walked downstairs to the kitchen. I saw a thin, clear glass vase with one single rose sitting on the wooden kitchen table. Attached to the rose is a tiny white envelope. I nervously opened it up, even though I knew it wasn't for me.

"Carol, can you please stay at your sister's house when you come up? I can't eat, I can't sleep. I just ask for some respect in our home. Love always, David."

I made sure to put the envelope back the same way I found it. Despite my dad's heartfelt plea, my mom continued to act precisely as she always had. She completely ignored his wishes and did just what she felt like doing.

Today, with age and hindsight, I recognize that my parent's relationship had nothing to do with me. Not that I wasn't affected but it was their business to work out, not mine. They were trying to figure it out the best way they knew how. We all just want to feel loved and that we belong. Maybe my mom felt like if she didn't stay at the house, she wouldn't belong to her tribe anymore and would lose her sense of belonging. I don't know, but at 17 years old, I only saw one side of my mom. I saw the side that lied, kept secrets and would do whatever she wanted, whenever she wanted, no matter who it hurt.

I was tired of the secrets; I was tired of the shame. I was ready to live my life on my own terms. In that way, I was a lot like my mom. I have a feeling she felt the same way at 17 as I did.

with Mamacita in Turks & Caicos

Chapter 10

PRESCRIBED BURN

On the day before I was to leave for West Virginia to visit Mom, I called my Aunt Rose. She picked up saying, "Hey Kate" and I could tell from her hushed tones she was at the hospital.

"Mommy's sleeping," she said. "She just wants to go home so the doctors will release her tomorrow."

I knew that meant the start of a hospice journey. I sucked in the air, held back those tears and said, "OK."

She continued in a more serious tone, "You and your dad should get down here. And call Aunt Millie. She might want you to pick her up." That's all I needed to hear. It felt like I had received my marching orders and it was now time to suit up for battle. The only thought or feeling that crossed my mind was, "I have to be there."

This was the phone call I had been waiting for the past year after leaving my apartment in New York City to live with Dad in New Jersey. The next morning, I got into my car, made sure all the doors were locked and raced through the ghettos of Patterson to pick up my Aunt Millie in her much safer neighborhood. We fueled up on Dunkin Donuts coffee and tried to get a handle on our current situation as we anxiously worked our way along the eight-hour journey to West Virginia.

As we merged onto I-78, I could feel butterflies in my stomach. My adrenaline surged. I took a deep breath, became cold and started to shake. My nervous system had moved into fight or flight mode.

When I finally got my feelings under control, I spoke my question out loud. "Aunt Millie, do you feel like mommy's cancer is… karma?" I couldn't believe I'd said it out loud.

"What do you mean?" Aunt Millie asked.

"The way she's treated my dad," I said.

I glanced across at my passenger. My Aunt Millie was staring out the window, not responding. I could feel the pit in my stomach. I was still shaking.

"She has cancer in the ovaries. Do you think maybe it's because she cheated on my dad?" I was determined to get an answer and gripped the steering wheel until my knuckles turned white.

My aunt sucked in a breath of air. "Well, what your mom chooses to do with her life is none of my business," she finally said. I saw the wisdom in those words. No matter who you are to someone, what a person chooses to do with their life is really none of your business.

My grandmother raised nine kids belonging to three different men entirely by herself on "the smell of an oily rag" as they say in Australia, which means the absolute minimum. All they had was each other, so they believed you never turn your back on family, no matter what. My mom's side of the family holds that belief firmly to this day.

At that time, I was unaware that somebody else's karma journey was not open for discussion. It is strictly between the person and the higher force that karma is connected to, but I felt justified to ask the question.

So I kept on. "You know, she ripped apart our family. She left her husband for her dead sister's husband and then got an abortion with his baby. And she never let my dad go, she never divorced him. That kind of karma surely has a return to sender stamp."

Aunt Millie kept staring out the window, saying nothing.

I continued. Now that I was finally ready to open up, I couldn't stop. I was letting my darkest, most horrible thoughts out into the world.

"Or, what if it's my fault? There were so many times I wished that she wasn't my mom," I said, feeling sick. "I used to tell her I hated her all the time and that we'd be so much better off without her." I began to cry.

"What if I manifested this?" Now I was sobbing.

Aunt Millie blew out her breath, exasperated. "Oh, stop Katie. You're not God or an evil witch casting spells on people, you don't have that kind of power." I felt a sense of relief for a second before the more powerful feeling of shame washed over me.

Cancer was nobody's fault. My teenage self might have been upset with my mom, but deep down I knew I was upset with myself for acting out toward her all those times. For being unable to regulate my own emotions and express myself more authentically. I didn't need to forgive her, I needed to forgive myself. She was doing her best with what she was given. As was I.

After eight hours on the highway followed by winding country roads, my Aunt Millie and I arrived at my West Virginia childhood home, if you can call a trailer with a half-done extension on it a home. The house my mom now shared with Eddie. The trailer was pretty much the same as when I'd lived there as a kid, though the built-on extension was almost finished. She had been working on it for 16 years.

It was pitch dark. The car bottomed out in the same spot in the familiar driveway, and the bump seemed to bring back all my childhood feelings of shame, frustration and desperation to flee.

I got out of the car, slamming the door shut behind me. It was a balmy summer night. The smell of a campfire in the air filled with the sounds of frogs and cicadas. Lightning bugs zipped past us with more stars in the sky than I could ever remember seeing. You don't see many stars in New York City, which should have brought *some* good feelings; however, all I could think about was how much I hated living there.

That hate quickly turned to remorse. I had only been back to this place three times in the past eight years. Why didn't I come to see her? I was only two hours away while in college at West Virginia University. She loved having me home. I could have made more of an effort. Regret washed over me.

As we walked toward the door, the peaceful night sounds were drowned out by a loud television and screaming kids. I imagined that, as usual, there were more heads than beds - typical of our family gatherings.

I opened the door and it only took a moment to take it all in. My Aunt Rose was in the kitchen, talking loudly on the phone to someone and Eddie was sitting watching television. My brother's kids were arguing over matchbox cars in the playroom.

My mom was slumped over on the couch, curled into herself like a ball, a puke bucket wrapped tightly in her left arm. I ran straight for the bathroom without even saying hello.

I stood in the bathroom with the water running, gasping for breath, trying to get my composure. It wasn't so much the cacophony of noise from kids fighting, the TV blaring, the phone calls and intense activity. It was that despite all the chaos going on around her, my mom didn't even flinch. That's how out of it she was. It hit me. My mom was going to die.

I started sobbing uncontrollably in my small childhood bathroom decorated characteristically by Mom – hunter-green wallpaper from floor to ceiling with a scenic bear border through the middle. The bear soap dispenser and embroidered hand towels matched the brown bears in the forest scene. She loved themes and was a true artist when it came to decorating. Every detail had to match (you should have seen Christmas). When I finally got myself together, I vowed: no more tears.

I blew my nose, stared at my glassy eyes and red swollen face as I said to myself, "You have to stay strong for her. She'll get upset if she sees you cry. Stay strong." I walked out of the bathroom and for the next 40 days she was alive, I kept my promise.

Later that evening I held the pink pan when she started to get sick and puke.

When I finally headed to my room for sleep, I noticed nothing had been touched. Cheetah, leopard and zebra print covered the comforter, pillows and picture frames. Even my hairdryer. Clearly, Mom had passed down her love of a theme. I sat gently on the bed, reluctant to wrinkle the bed cover. The room felt like a shrine waiting for me to come home. But even though I was there now, it didn't feel like home.

∼

The next day, I was tense waiting for my dad to arrive. I washed the dishes and worried about what would happen with him and Eddie under the same roof. But I had nothing to worry about. Whether time had healed old wounds, or my mom's illness had put any bad feelings into perspective, when my dad walked in, Eddie stood up from the worn leather couch where he'd been sitting next to my mom and shook my dad's hand. They talked about the drive, how long it took, and where Dad stopped off for gas, and that was that.

My mom was happy to see my dad. She opened her eyes and reached out her hand when she heard his voice. He walked over, squatted down in front of the couch, and took her thin hand gently in his own. When he leaned in and kissed her on the cheek, she beamed up at him. A bit of her old self shone through her gaunt face.

During the last days of my mom's life, no one talked about how strange their relationship was. Or how odd it was to have my dad and Eddie in the same house. Or how Eddie might have felt that my mom turned to my dad to organize all her affairs, even though she'd been with Eddie for nine years.

There wasn't much down time for anybody to stew. It was always a full house. Only five beds, but there were at least ten people there at any given time, adults and children. Plus, all the random people who stopped by to say goodbye. My mom had four brothers, four sisters, five children, six grandchildren and sixteen nieces and nephews, plus their kids. Being the second eldest of nine and the first girl born, she raised all her brothers and sisters and helped them with their children. She was a mom to us all.

∼

That night, my Aunt Rose, Aunt Millie and I were on night duty. My mom was sleeping on the couch. She'd only been home a little more than 48 hours so she didn't have all the equipment that would come later. I was sitting in the kitchen with my aunts when we heard her calling out.

I stood up quickly, pushing the chair back across the linoleum floor.

"We're here, Mom," I said. "What do you need?"

"I need to go to the bathroom," she said. She was struggling to sit up.

"Hold on, we'll take you," I said. I called out to my aunts.

Aunt Rose hustled into the room, her head awry, Aunt Millie close behind her.

"She needs to go to the bathroom," I said. "Can you help me?" I was already moving around behind to help her up.

Between the three of us, we managed to get her up and off the couch. She was heavy and awkward to move. She couldn't support herself much at all. We struggled with her into the bathroom and were helping her onto the toilet. Suddenly she collapsed, all of her deadweight tumbling right on top of tiny, 90-pound Aunt Millie who started to fall back into the bathtub. I panicked, left my aunts with my mom and ran for my dad, yelling at him to come and help us. He sat straight up in the bed – he's a light sleeper. I ran back to my mom and waited for my dad to come and help us. It took him longer than I expected.

Later he told me, "I literally couldn't move, Kate. I felt like an elephant was standing on my chest. I thought I was having a heart attack."

After that night, my mom was completely bedridden with an oxygen tank. My aunts and I took turns on diaper and bath duty, and I spent my days watching my mom, my rock, become utterly helpless and completely dependent on others.

I felt hopeless, but at the same time so thankful that I could participate in midwifing her through this transition. There was absolutely nowhere else I wanted to be. And for her last days, I stayed almost exclusively by her side.

I sat on the couch, in the living room where my mom lay in her hospice bed. I watched *House Hunters International* and *Love it or List it*. It was my way of mentally travelling around the globe without having to leave that room physically. The television channel, HGTV was on 24/7. I would help my mom with whatever she needed. She wasn't eating much, but whenever she would get a craving for something, someone would be rushing out to get that for her. Once it was orange soda. Another time cherry tomatoes with Italian dressing yet it didn't last, as soon as it went down it came right back up.

My aunts and I made sure she kept up with her meds, despite mom not believing in medications. None of us ever took antibiotics or went to the doctor growing up, so my mother could only be convinced to take the liquid pain killer. She called it the "tap tap" because we would give her two taps at a time on her tongue.

'Tap tap' was a pain killer prescribed to people with migraines, so I can't imagine it was strong enough to help with the pain she was experiencing, but she refused to take the morphine. She was still coherent; she knew what was going on. Once she took the morphine her body would get comfortable enough to quit fighting and shut down. She had a high threshold for pain and was fighting for her life. The nurses were astounded by just how much fight she had in her.

There would be times when I struggled to hold back tears.

She'd get feisty and claim she was going to get out of that bed. "Just you wait and see," she said. Of course, she never did.

Once she woke up from a deep sleep and looked over at me.

"Katie," she said. "I saw God."

I turned to look at her. She sat upright with her bald head and oxygen tubes up her nose.

She nodded at me as if to reiterate her point. "God," she said. "He went around my body like a clock. He shined a light onto each part of my body where the number of the clock would be. When he got to number 12, I knew."

'Knew what?" I asked her.

"I knew it was OK to go," she said.

I didn't know what to say about that. It was so beautiful yet incredibly sad. Even though she wasn't religious, I believe my mom felt closer to God the closer she came to death. Because a few hours later she asked me, "When am I going to see Meg? She's my most spiritual friend?"

Guess who showed up that day, unexpected and unannounced? Meg, Dan's better half.

She had so many good days and some that were awful. One day she would call me her angel. But the next day she'd tell me how bad she felt for Justin, the guy I was dating at the time, for having to "put up with me." But most of the time she just slept. And so did I. She barely ate a thing, nor did I. She never left her bed and I never left the house. She spent her awake time being visited by friends who came to say goodbye. And I spent my awake time isolating myself from everyone I knew. She was withering away – and in so many ways, I was too.

with Alicia at
Dance School Recital

Chapter 11

HOTSPOT

My dear friend Alicia was getting married, and I was to be a bridesmaid. Alicia was more like family than a friend. We'd grown up together. We were in the same kindergarten class and lived just two blocks from each other until I moved to West Virginia. Her mom and my mom were great friends, and I remember long afternoons when my mom would perm her great-grandmother's hair while Alicia and I flipped through issues of TigerBeat gushing over Leonardo DiCaprio.

"I don't want to go," I said to Mom, putting down the protein shake I was trying to get her to drink with a straw. "I really don't."

"No," my mom said. "You need to go. She's counting on you." My mom's voice was soft and shaky but firm. She shifted a little to one side and I saw her wince in pain.

"I don't want to go without you," I said.

"Take Justin. He wants to go with you."

I started to speak, but she interrupted, "No. Go." She closed her eyes. The conversation had taken all her strength.

My mom was supposed to be my plus one at Alicia's wedding. Given the state she was in, she was too sick to go, so I took Justin. I'm not exactly sure why, but she was adamant about me buying two cards for Alicia. One from me and one from herself. She was always a big card giver and that day she managed to write a shaky but legible message.

"Dear Alicia, I'm so glad you and Katie have each other. I hope you and Katie raise children together just like me and your mother did. Love always, Carol."

Before I left, I went in to see her and said goodbye. I bent down to kiss her cold but still plump lips and placed my hand on her bald patchy head. I got close to her face, now you could see the shape of her skull under her pale skin. I took a big breath to hold back my tears.

"I love you. I'll see you on Sunday," I said.

She smiled, her face completely transforming when she did. And for a moment I saw my mom again and I believed, with a child's belief, that everything would be just fine. "Okay honey," she said. "I love you too. Be careful, drive safely and tell everyone I said hello."

Did I know that was the last time I would ever speak to my mother? Yes, I suppose part of me did. But so much of me believed that we still had time. That there would be a moment where I could say the things I wanted to say, and ask her the questions I needed answers to. But it was time to go for both her and me.

∼

I don't remember much of the wedding except that I didn't touch my food (which is usually the best part) and when a particularly annoying song like "Call Me, Maybe" came on, I snuck outside for a cigarette. I wanted to be in the moment, but I felt restless and unsettled. Alicia could see that I wasn't alright, but she didn't expect me to do much more than be with her. I could barely manage that and after a while, I picked a big argument with Justin.

The next day, we tried to mend our messy fight on the two-hour car ride back to Justin's apartment in Brooklyn. I was in no place to mend anything, but I also wasn't in a good place to lose anyone else. In the end, we made up. I remember how striking the full harvest moon looked in the dusk sky as we crossed over the Williamsburg Bridge.

The original plan was for me to drop Justin off at his apartment and then make my way back to West Virginia to be with my mom. But as I pulled up in front of Justin's apartment, I found a great parking place (a rare gem in Bed-Stuy) and Justin said, "It's getting late Babe, and you're so tired. I don't think you should drive another eight hours by yourself."

I felt depleted. I had nothing left to give, not even an argument and it felt nice to have someone take care of me for a minute. In the end, I decided he was right. I would leave in the morning after a good night's sleep.

That was my last "good night's sleep". The next morning, I got that call from Dad. My mom was gone. This time, forever.

∼

My mom didn't want a wake or funeral. When we talked about it, she'd say, "No. No funeral. No wake." But she wouldn't explain why, and we didn't want to upset her. I wonder if she didn't want people to make a "fuss" because she accepted death and knew it was just a part of life. Or was she carrying around so much shame that she didn't feel she was worth the time, effort, energy, and money that goes into a remembrance? We'll never really know her reason but Dad still organized a wake so the family could pay their respects.

The viewing was held at a tiny white funeral parlor in the small country town of Clay, West Virginia, the same town where I went to middle school and high school. It felt like a movie set, seeing her lips glued shut, dressed in the pale-yellow dress she'd worn to Dee's wedding. She looked peaceful in her short blonde wig, more rested in that casket than the images I had burned into my memory from the past few weeks of caring for her. I touched her cold hands and closed my eyes, praying, wishing I could have more time with her. I would have done anything for one more conversation.

Like my mom, I insisted that none of my friends come to WV or make a "big deal" of it. It was just family. A few girlfriends from school showed up, including my besties Renae and Lynn. We sat together a few rows back from my mom's open casket.

Renae gazed forward, lowered her head and whispered, "Kate, remember that time we were trying to sneak out of your house in the middle of the night and your mom caught us?"

"Yea," Lynn added. "She came in and was like, 'Girls, why don't you just go through the front door!? You know I don't care if you want to go out. C'mon I thought someone was trying to break in, Jesus Christ.'" Lynn stifled a giggle, and I felt a smile creep across my face.

"Or that time we came home and your mom had all your bongs and alcohol bottles lined up on the counter," Renae said. 'She was laughing at us."

"She didn't even say anything as we walked back into your bedroom with all the gear in our hands," Lynn finished. "If that were my parents, I wouldn't have been allowed out of the house ever again!"

"Yeah, me neither. You know how my dad is." Renae said.

As I sat there in my loose black dress, on one of the worst days of my life, suddenly, I was flooded with admiration and gratitude for my mom. I might have questioned her personal life choices but she was the coolest when it came to being a mom. She genuinely trusted me. She had faith I could make responsible decisions and when I didn't, she was there, accepting all of me, unconditionally. Her life and spirit were a canvas; so much larger than the few unpleasant brush strokes I chose to focus on. She did her best with what she'd been given and with her own level of awareness as a mom, daughter, sister, aunt, friend and wife. Who am I to judge?

I thought about all the things she embedded into my DNA, consciously and probably more unconsciously, like don't waste your precious time worrying about what other people think, mind your own business, never, ever believe you are better than anyone, and have fun because life is too short! These morals would stay with me forever.

I felt the tears fall again. I was so grateful to have had her as my mom. And thankful to my oldest friends for reminding me of that.

~

My dad and I were the last ones to leave the room. As we sat there together, gazing at the casket, I tried to put myself in his shoes. If I had mixed emotions, I couldn't imagine what he was going through. They raised five children together and were still legally married even though he had been abandoned by her more than once.

She had lied, cheated and broken his heart, but I knew that he still loved her. He would have done anything for her. She was the mother of his children and through everything, even when she treated him the worst, he never said one horrible thing about her. I could never fathom, at the time, how it felt to be so loyal, loving and devoted to anybody, or anything, for that matter.

∼

After a few days, I packed up the meagre stuff I'd accumulated during the time I'd been in West Virginia and loaded my car. As per my mom's last wishes, my dad was to live on the land himself instead of selling it. Even though my mom had been with Eddie for almost a decade, she'd turned to my dad in her last days. A team to the end.

I headed back to New Jersey, to the big, empty family home. I went back to work and tried to return my life to normal.

It was bizarre going back to reality after locking myself away from the world for eight weeks. I wasn't sure what the grieving process was supposed to look like, so I went on like usual. I was going through the motions when a few weeks later, Hurricane Sandy hit the east coast. The news was filled with advice about what to do, where to go and how to navigate following a natural disaster. I didn't want to get trapped in my house in New Jersey alone with no power and potential flooding, so I went to Justin's place in Brooklyn.

Hurricane Sandy was a catastrophe. Over eight million people were left without power and the subway systems were shut due to flooding. Instead of feeling safe and secure, I felt helpless and trapped in someone else's home. First at my mom's, now at Justin's. With all that was happening around me, I didn't have time alone to process recent events, but if I couldn't help myself, I could try to help someone else so I volunteered at a warehouse in Williamsburg packing boxes of supplies for flood victims.

Justin was wanting to make our relationship work, but I needed space. He could tell I was pulling away and I was honest that I didn't know what I wanted. Around this time, I also had some email exchanges with Finn. I told him about my mom's passing and he told me about his around the world travel plans that included a stop in America with Sarah. I suggested we meet up, but Finn turned me down. A wise decision, in retrospect.

I forgot to close the browser of my email on Justin's computer, and he confronted me about this email with Finn. I denied it meant anything, but it wasn't long after that I suggested we go on a "break."

While me and Justin were on this break, I went out with a friend for happy hour. Before long, it was midnight and I didn't realize they'd closed the PATH train back to Jersey. I swallowed my pride and called Justin to see if I could sleep over.

"Hey Justin, "I said. "I didn't realize they closed the PATH train at night for construction." I paused to gather my thoughts. I was pretty drunk. "Can I come over?"

Justin paused. Even through my drunken fog, I could tell he didn't want me coming over.

"No, you're only using me to crash, and you're drunk. I don't want you here," he said

"No. I'm really stuck," I said, desperate.

"OK, fine. But you have to sleep on the couch and I'm throwing all of your stuff out on the street."

"Sure, sure," I said. I thought he was being dramatic.

I grabbed the next taxi to his place in Brooklyn, and when I got out of the taxi, I saw that he'd left all my stuff in a black trash bag in front of his place. I let myself into the apartment. It was dark and Justin's bedroom door was locked. After attempting to open it, I realized he wasn't kidding. I made my way to the couch, but shortly after, my sleep was interrupted by Justin. Following a heated exchange, I finally ended up passing out on his couch, utterly exhausted.

Early the next day with the black garbage bag slung over my shoulder, I hailed a taxi to the PATH train and made my way back to my house in Jersey.

My house was empty, my relationship was over, my mom was gone. It was time to start new fires.

In Loving Memory
Carol Delimon
<3

When I come to the end of the road,
and the sun has set for me,
I want no rites in gloom-filled rooms.
Why cry for a soul set Free?
Miss me a little, but not too long,
and not with your head bowed low;
Remember the love that we once shared.
Miss me, but let me go.
For this is a journey that we all must take,
and each must go alone.
It's all a part of the Master's plan.
A step on the road to home.
When you are lonely and sick at heart,
go to the friends we know, and bury your
sorrows in doing good deeds.

<3

Chapter 12

BURNING UP

It wasn't the best time to end things with Justin. We had already booked flights to Florida to spend the holidays with his family and some of mine. Now I would be spending the holidays alone and without my mom for the first time.

The most surreal part was going to the mailbox every day and pulling out both condolence and Christmas cards. It seemed wrong to be mourning at Christmas. Like I'd made a misstep in some way.

It was during that already awful holiday season that I found out that Finn was engaged to Sarah. According to Facebook, he'd popped the question while they were travelling overseas. In his pictures, they looked happy. I tried not to dwell on it but it was impossible. My heart hurt from all the loss.

I had the urge to dye my hair dark to match how I felt inside. So, on New Year's Eve, I bought the darkest shade of brown I could find. It was a two-for-one deal, and I needed the two boxes because my hair was so long.

None of my friends wanted to take on the responsibility. They knew it wasn't a good idea, so I did it myself in the bathtub. My friends were right, of course. It turned out blotchy with green-tinted ends, but I shook it off and went to a Brooklyn warehouse party where I danced all night in the dark so nobody noticed anyway.

Don't ask me how, but the next day as I was making the savage trip back to Jersey, switching trains in the west village, I got hustled out of $200, lightbulbs and cigarettes from a gypsy that I sat and had coffee with at a diner. She told me her psychic predictions for my future on a napkin. Only in New York City. After I got home from that strange encounter, I went into the bathroom, leaned on the small white countertop and gave myself a good look in the mirror. My BOGO (buy one get one) hair dye looked awful, I had makeup smudged around my eyes, I was coming down from the fun of last night, my mouth was dry, my head hurt and a gypsy had just conned me. I thought, is this how I want to start a *new* year?

Our family home in New Jersey went on the market soon after. With Dad still in West Virginia taking care of my mom's affairs, I was left to take care of the house in Jersey while we waited for it to sell. Every few weeks my dad would come up for a few days to sort through everything. What he didn't throw out he took back with him to West Virginia. Slowly, the house emptied around me.

As I watched my childhood home empty, I felt more and more hollow on the inside. None of my siblings were around to go through it with me. In some ways, I was the lucky one, able to say a proper goodbye to my childhood. But I also felt sad and lonely, without any of them there to experience the closing of a family chapter filled with so many memories. I also felt guilty that my dad had to handle all of it alone.

I knew the house would eventually sell, but I didn't know my next move. I felt secure at my job but had no job satisfaction. I didn't want to work in legal marketing and I didn't want to move back to New York City. I wanted to flee, but I didn't know what to do or where to go. All I knew was that I was sinking. I was past the brink of burnout.

∽

Yet, I stayed for another year, despite everything inside of me telling me to "LEAVE NEW YORK." I pushed those feelings down and continued my hedonistic lifestyle, doing the things I had become addicted to. Working. Travelling. Drinking. Drugs. Sex. I didn't invent those self-destructive habits, but I certainly embraced them.

Being self-destructive in New York was like wearing a badge of honor. Everybody I knew was doing the same things. Nobody showed they cared. Nobody worried about the effect those behaviors were having on them. And being and doing *everything* was the way everyone I knew was living. I was about to turn 27. I would joke about hoping *not* to join the '27 club' alongside rock stars Jim Morrison, Janis Joplin, Kurt Cobain and Amy Winehouse, the beautiful stars whose lights had burned out too young.

Not that I had to worry, my life was far from that of a rock star. I was having trouble sleeping at night on my single blow-up mattress in an empty house. Difficulty sleeping was not something I had ever had problems with before. It didn't help when a racoon got inside one night, scaring me half to death. I learned that the Police don't like to be called multiple times in the middle of the night for this type of thing. According to them, it was "not an emergency, ma'am."

After a couple of deals fell through, I started worrying about how long Dad would have to pay the mortgage. He was forced into early retirement because he couldn't find work in West Virginia, which wouldn't have been his preferred choice. I knew this had nothing to do with me but I felt protective of Dad and wanted his life to get better. I wanted him to focus on himself yet he was still sacrificing so much for my mom and her final wishes for him to live in West Virginia.

Not only was I emotionally burnt out but now my physical body began to fall apart. I started having digestive problems, cramps and stomach aches. My body reacted as though I was allergic to everything I ate. My belly was permanently bloated and swollen so much that my Aunt Millie asked if I was pregnant once. Doctors said it was standard IBS, GI issues or maybe a leaky gut and would just take time to heal. Never once did a doctor ask about stress or my lifestyle choices so I never got to the root cause and couldn't remedy my stomach issues for years.

Compounding this, I kept getting throat infections. I went to multiple doctors and specialists. I tried every kind of diet and took every piece of advice I was given. Nothing helped. In hindsight, my lifestyle wasn't helping, but I lacked the will to douse the flames. I was lost and running out of choices. I had to make drastic changes.

∼

One Monday in late May, I had an idea of what that change could look like. I went to the Chief Marketing Officer and asked if I could be "let go." To his credit, he didn't laugh me out of his office. Instead, he just leaned back in his chair, and said, "I can't do that, Katie." He shook his head to emphasize his point.

"I get it," I said, standing up. I kicked the chair leg, not out of frustration but in my haste to get out of his office. But I wasn't giving up. I went straight into Human Resources and asked them directly to lay me off.

Those in earshot were surprised. It wasn't every day someone asked to be fired, but in the end, they couldn't help me either.

So, I decided to take a different approach and since my direct manager was away, I thought it would be a great opportunity to enjoy my lunchtime. Tuesday and Wednesday I met my Australian friend, Carter at the basement Irish pub across the street. We drank watermelon martinis while rain poured down. The sun came out on Thursday, so Amanda and I sat outside at a small restaurant in Tribeca, gulping down wine like it was cold refreshing water. I felt no shame.

In the late afternoon, I would go back into the office, blatantly drunk. I spent the rest of each afternoon making stupid jokes and texting Amanda. My co-workers watched me with sidelong glances from behind their computer monitors, but still, nothing happened.

I needed to try harder. That Friday I didn't shower and went to work without a bra or makeup. I wore a long black sundress with bright green and purple flowers, my knee-high Hunter rain boots and tied my hair in a messy bun on the top of my head. It was not acceptable office attire and a far cry from my usual black dress pants, crisp blouse and high heels. Honestly, if I had a pink wig, I would have worn it.

A co-worker came to my desk to request the key to the marketing closet. I was busy stacking all the office supplies I had into a little tower, but the alligator clips were flatly refusing to do what I wanted. I looked up at him as the whole thing tumbled down littering my desk and the floor around me with paper clips, pencils, pens, alligator clips and post-it notes.

"Katie, is everything all right?" he asked, his forehead wrinkled in concern.

I smirked and raised my voice a bit too many notches so people around could hear. "Me? I'm fiiiiiine. I'm great. I feel liberated!" I laughed again.

People around me were staring but then quickly looked away. I saw myself through their eyes. A crazy, half-drunk, 20-something motherless woman who was finally, truly, losing her shit. I could physically feel the screws loosening in my head. What was I doing?

Just before the end of the day, the CMO popped over to my desk.

"Katie, can you come to see me in my office, please?" he asked in his thick New York accent. It wasn't a request.

"Certainly," I said, brushing crumbs from an afternoon muffin off my sundress. I mooched after him along the hallway feeling elated. I was finally getting fired! Now I had a reason to leave New York City and I could start my escapades.

I sat on the leather chair across from his wooden desk and waited for him to speak.

He sat down on the edge of the desk rather than in the chair behind and smiled. I frowned a little in response. Do people usually smile when they're firing you?

"Katie, we've been aware that you haven't been happy for some time." He paused waiting for me to speak. I said nothing, just watched him. He was still smiling.

"We value your contribution to our company and believe you have more to offer, more than you're doing." My frown deepened. This didn't sound good.

"So, we've created a new role for you on Sam's team – event coordinator." His smile had widened even further. He leaned back a little, waiting for me to speak.

I was shocked. Had he missed my performance of the past week? "I don't know what to say," I said because I really didn't know what to say.

He must have taken that as a positive sign because he launched straight into the details of the job. It involved travelling around the United States and assisting with dinners and events. I'd stay in Ritz Carlton's, and get a 20% raise in addition to all my travel, accommodation and expenses covered.

On paper, it seemed like a dream job.

I took it as a sign. I should be sticking it out in New York. I should make this new job and lifestyle work.

From a rational perspective, it made sense. I was young, I had a great job where the people undoubtedly loved me, great friends and family in the area, and decent savings with no debt. Once the house in Jersey sold, I could get an apartment and start climbing the corporate ladder. Again.

I sighed. My CMO was looking at me expectantly.

I smiled brightly and stood up, thrusting my hand out to him. "Sounds great," I said. "I'm looking forward to seeing what I can bring to the position." I shook his hand and left the office.

I took the new role despite a sinking feeling in my stomach. It was the sign I was looking for and it made sense, yet the voice inside saying *leave New York City* wouldn't stop whispering.

∼

Corporate travel is nothing like traveling for pleasure. It's the opposite. Hosting awards dinners for staid, uptight lawyers who often seem like they have better things to do is a surefire way to erode your soul. My evening would consist of spending three hours working the room talking to people about the local area (awful), the awards they were nominated for (boring) or their work (truly mind-numbing).

The hours slipped away. Then days. Then weeks. The time I would never get back. Time spent doing things I cared nothing about. Talking to people who would be in my life for a few unimportant moments before slipping away completely unnoticed. I would never think about them again. And vice versa.

I needed clarity, and the way I found clarity was by travelling. Not soul-sucking corporate travel, but the kind of travel that expands your mind, and opens you up to new explorations, possibilities and people.

I spent my nights sitting cross-legged on hotel beds in Miami, Las Vegas or New Orleans, trolling the internet for inspiration. Before long, I stumbled on a $99 one-way flight from West Virginia to Honolulu departing the first week of December. It felt like the answer I was looking for, or at least just a pleasant deviation until the answer became clear. I sent a silent plea to the universe that everything would come together and booked it.

It was only a few weeks later that a friend from Australia, Dennis, sent me a message. He was visiting New York City for a few days. We met up in Brooklyn at the Alligator Lounge where they serve free pizza with every beer.

It was mid-week so the bar was dead, just a handful of other people drinking beer and having an early feed while Bob Marley played in the background. We ordered our beer and pizza and sat outside at a wobbly wooden table. When the beers arrived, we both drank, I ate Dennis's pizza as well as mine, and I told him my plan.

He took another deep swallow of beer and asked, "Why don't you come back to Australia?"

"I'd love to but I can only get a visiting visa and I've already been to Australia. I want to see places I haven't seen before," I said, concentrating on my pizza.

"What if I can get you a visa to stay longer?" He brushed his hand through his short, buzz-cut hair. "Would you want to work for my travel company? We sponsor visas all the time."

"What?" I said. "Really? Of course! That sounds awesome and perfect for me." I grabbed him in a one-armed hug, but then pulled back. "Wait, are you serious? Do you really think you can help me?"

Dennis said, "Of course, I'm serious. I'm having brunch with my business partner tomorrow. Why don't you come with me? You can meet him and we can sort out the details."

This was it! This was my way out of my dismal, soul-wrenching job. I was thrilled. I hugged him again as I was overly excited.

"OK, awesome!" he said with just as much excitement.

Brunch went great and the visa seemed like a pretty straightforward process. So, I tacked onto my one-way ticket from West Virginia to Hawaii a one-way ticket from Hawaii to Sydney for Christmas Day.

The Jersey house sold that summer and it felt like things were falling into place, however, relief was tempered by worry for Dad. After paying a mortgage for thirty years having sacrificed so much, he walked away with nothing. I was concerned for his future.

If that wasn't bad enough, his only sister passed away that Father's Day. He wasn't able to see her before she passed because he was in West Virginia. I guess in a way I was in mourning for him as well.

I moved out of the house and into an apartment in Brooklyn for two months. Then I moved in with Amanda and her family in New Jersey until I left for Hawaii. I downsized my life with each move until what was left would fit into two average-sized suitcases.

I kept nothing I didn't need and left nothing behind to come back to. I was leaving behind my time in New York City and so much of my identity. It was the end of an era.

∼

I arrived in Hawaii with two suitcases and dreams of a new life. But things didn't work out as I'd hoped.

The beautiful, tropical island was full of vacationing families and honeymooners. Everywhere you looked moms bounced chubby babies in the pool's shallow end, and couples locked arms while splashing in the surf.

I wanted to share these beautiful places with someone, instead, my companion was the constant feeling of loneliness. I wanted to point out the dolphins passing by or grab a beer while the sun sunk over the blue-green sea. I couldn't help but wonder if I was making the right decision. New York City had always been my dream. Always. The thought crept in – was I running to something or *from* something?

I'd only been in Hawaii a few days, staying on the North Shore watching the Pipeline Competition, when I decided to head down to the southeast side of Hanauma Bay to do some snorkeling. I thought I could rely on the public transport system. After all, it's a tiny island. How bad could it be?

I ended up waiting three hours for the bus to arrive and then it took me another two hours to get to Waikiki central station. By the time I finally arrived it was dark and nobody could tell me the right bus to get on. In frustration, I got off at a random bus stop and hailed a taxi, which was hard to do when you're used to New York City. I managed to get one and the driver asked me to direct him. I'd gotten the approximate address but of course, I didn't know my way around the island. It turns out that neither did the driver. We ended up lost with neither of us knowing where to go and my phone dead.

It shouldn't have been a big deal, but I found myself crying in the back of the taxi, saying to the driver, "You're supposed to tell me where to go. You're supposed to know!"

Perhaps it wasn't the directionless driver making me feel lost and confused, but the sense that my life compass was off-center.

I'd just uprooted my life and taken a chance on the unknown. I'd always believed that "Not all those who wander are lost," but this time was different. I felt I was seeking something rather than just enjoying a ride.

I needed to pull myself together. Going back wasn't an option. There was only a forward motion and even though I was moving physically forward, it soon became clear I wasn't moving forward emotionally. I sent Finn an email. In my mind, I thought, "We're friends, right? Why not reach out and tell him I'm going to be in Australia?" He was engaged and probably planning a wedding at that very moment, but friends meet up when they're in town, right?

I suggested meeting up and Finn was keen. He said it would be nice to see me and asked me to get in touch once I settled. In no time flat, I started to have visions of us reuniting. We couldn't deny our connection. We just had to be on the same continent.

I was not only getting anxious to move on and see Finn, but I still hadn't received my visa to get into Australia. The morning of my flight, I received an email from Dennis with the visa attached explaining that it was only active for 90 days, not the year we'd thought.

There was nothing he could do and I understood that these things happen, but I was shaken up. This wasn't the plan I had in my head after packing up my entire life. Ninety days was hardly enough time to start a whole life over.

First things first. I just had to get on the plane.

Chapter 13

BUSHFIRE

I landed in Sydney on Christmas Day and made my way through immigration, baggage claims and customs. I was exhausted. In Hawaii, I had come down with another throat infection. A regular occurrence but it didn't make it any less intense. It came with a high fever and patchy white sores in the throat. It hurt to swallow, burned to talk and made me feel completely wiped out. My dad said my mom used to get them all the time, too.

As I walked out of the airport's double doors where families waited for loved ones, hauling my two suitcases that represented all the possessions I had in the world, I felt despondent.

It will never be Christmas to me in hot, humid weather. I waited at the airport curb for Dennis and Ali, even though I wasn't mentally in the best place, I slapped a smile on. I was back in one of my favorite places in the world, and about to be reunited with some of my most treasured friendships.

The next day I hit the road with friends, including Ali and Dennis. We were headed to Byron Bay for a New Year's festival.

Although my body needed rest, there wasn't much of that going on so I partied through it, determined to enjoy my time in Australia and ignore my problems. When we returned to Sydney, Ali and Dennis let me crash on a blow-up mattress in their spare bedroom while I figured out what to do next.

I started work at the travel company and immediately felt out of place. The job was to sell travel packages to backpackers. It was very competitive. The company sat side by side with competing businesses, literally pulling people off the streets. It was immediately apparent that I was in over my head. Dennis said, "It's like you become a deer in headlights when it comes to following through with the sale." He was right, I just froze.

There's an art to sales and I didn't have the skills. More importantly, I didn't have the passion for becoming skillful. Not only had I let myself down, but I'd also let Dennis down and made him look bad to his business partner. He'd taken a big chance on me. This job was based purely on sales and I just wasn't cutting it. And then I had to come home each day and sleep in his spare bedroom. My bruised ego felt like an inadequate child.

I spent those three months as an adult orphan going from one friend's couch to another with no home nor direction. Things were not working out the way I had imagined. Perhaps I had made the wrong decision coming to Australia.

∼

Tonight was the night I was going to see Finn again. He invited me to meet up after work for drinks and to check out a friend's pop-up art gallery.

Somehow, I still felt like a giddy little girl with her first crush. What should I wear? What will I say? How will he act? I tried on outfit after outfit while Ali popped in and out giving me advice.

I finally settled on a sheer, cream-sleeveless top with blue studs on the collar and skinny jeans with the skyline of New York printed on them. I didn't have any shoes that worked, so I stopped in and bought a comfortable pair of nude wedges just before meeting up at a pub on Oxford Street.

Finn arrived on his motorcycle as I walked up the street, and when our eyes met my stomach fizzed. Time slowed. He was wearing a white T-shirt with black jeans. His sandy blond hair was longer than I had seen before – down to his ears. It swished to the side when he swung his head out of his bike helmet.

"Hey Katie," Finn said, with a slow smile, and I knew: I was more attracted to him than ever.

We sat down and ordered a beer. It felt like no time has passed. We talked about our recent travels, my plans (or lack thereof) and my awful job.

"So, what's happening with you? Any plans to travel soon?" I asked Finn. I was on my second cider and feeling good.

"Sarah is travelling for work right now, but we'll plan something when she gets back," Finn said.

"Oh," I said, taken off guard. "How is Sarah?" I asked, rallying quickly. No need for him to see how I was feeling.

"She's OK," he said. "Busy with work."

"And how are the wedding plans?" Part of me didn't want to know, but more of me was desperate to hear the details.

Finn didn't answer. Just rolled his eyes and grimaced. I let the subject go, but I couldn't help wondering if that meant trouble in paradise.

"It's getting late. Should we head out?" I said, to change the subject.

"Yep," he said, smiling. "Let's go."

The art gallery was nearby, so we walked. It was small, and a few of Finn's friends were there. As much as I was enjoying his attention and that he wasn't gushing about his relationship, I couldn't help but feel awkward. What did all these people think about me, I wondered. What does Sarah think?

We'd seen every piece of art twice when Finn asked, "Should we get out of here and grab another drink?"

"Definitely," I replied immediately. I didn't want the night to end and I couldn't help thinking, what are we doing? We've never been just friends, and he knows I still have feelings. Is he pulling at my heartstrings on purpose? But the louder voice said, don't ask questions, just stay in the moment.

We had another drink, and before I knew it Finn was hugging me goodbye. The night was over. Nothing happened. He made some noise about catching up again before I left, but as much as I hoped that was true, no plans were made. He walked me to the bus stop, and I stayed calm as I waited for the bus to take me back to my blow-up mattress in the southern hemisphere.

It felt like I was being held in reserve. I couldn't figure out his motivation for wanting to spend an evening with me, but I didn't dare say anything to his face. When the bus arrived, I climbed on board and gave a happy little wave.

Once I was home, I tossed and turned, unable to sleep from wondering if there could be more. So, like an addict needing another hit, I grabbed my phone and wrote him an email.

The next morning, I woke up to his reply. He said it was nice to see me, but he was busy for the next few weeks and hoped I enjoyed the remainder of my time in Australia.

A shame-hole opened and into it, I fell. I was mortified I'd written to him in the first place, gushing about how good of a night it was and that I didn't want to step on any toes but would love (LOVE!) to see him again. Ugh. Why had I left myself so vulnerable? I had known what his response would be and now, here it was. Black and white. I had to respect his position. It was time for me to move on.

∼

The last week I was in Australia, Amanda flew over and we spent my 28th birthday at McKenzie's beach drinking champagne, swimming, laughing, seeing friends and petting every dog that went by.

At the end of the day, we packed up our stuff and started walking home. "It's been a pretty amazing day," I said, slinging my arm around Amanda's neck.

She squeezed me back. "Yep! And I'm only a little bit drunk!"

"I'm going to be sad to leave," I said, "especially without seeing Finn again."

"Ah. You're bummed?" She asked, bumping her hip into mine as we walked along. I couldn't help but smile. And as I looked up, there he was. Finn. Standing in the same spot where he and I had met for the first night five years ago.

If this wasn't some kind of sign from the universe then I don't know what is.

"How strange seeing you here again. Same place," I said, making a wide sweeping gesture with my arm.

"Maybe it's fate," he laughed. Amanda bumped her hip against mine again.

"You remember my wife, Amanda, aka Delicious?" I asked.

"Of course, how could I forget," he said. "Good to see you again."

"Sooo good to see you!" Amanda said. She pulled her arm from around my neck and pulled Finn into a big hug. "You know it's Katie's birthday, right?"

"Of course, I know. Happy birthday." I suddenly felt warm inside but I was annoyed he didn't send me a message, so I flipped him the bird and he just laughed at me.

"Why don't you come out with us tonight," I asked in a rush. "We're just heading out for some birthday drinks at the Beaver."

"Sounds good," he said. He popped his helmet onto his head as my own heart gave a flip. "I'll see you there," he said, giving us a little wave as he headed back toward his bike.

Amanda looked at me, her eyes alight. "It's fate," she said. "Oh my god, I can't believe we were just talking about him!" I couldn't believe it either. And I couldn't wait for the evening to arrive.

∽

It was like déjà vu – me, Finn, Amanda and the same group of friends I had when I was living in Bondi, all sitting around having some laughs over beers. Finn looked great and every time our eyes met; I couldn't help but smile. It was just like old times.

I wanted so badly for this to be my reality again. I wanted to be staying here and spending time with Finn. But I had to accept that it wasn't. I couldn't stay. When I got in the car to go to dinner, Amanda asked how I felt seeing Finn this time and tears filled my eyes.

I said, "I'm still heartbroken after all these years."

"Oh Scrum. I know," Amanda said. She put her head on my shoulder.

I sniffled. "I want to stay. I want to be able to see what's there," I said. "But I can't."

Amanda didn't say anything. Just squeezed my hand.

It was like everything I dreamed of was there right in front of my eyes but it wasn't actually real.

I did meet up with Finn one more time before I left, for a quick breakfast at Lamrock Café on the corner of Campbell Parade in Bondi. We sat outside and looked out over the ocean while we talked. It felt like every word was filled with meaning, but at the same time, it felt like we weren't saying anything at all.

We'd finished up our food and coffee and as we were making moves to leave, I put my hand on his arm.

"Think you'll ever travel to the States again," I asked, keeping my voice light.

"Ahh, probably not. Been there, done that, you know?" Finn said. I felt my hopes slip away. I was still holding onto the idea we could have a romantic reunion in the future.

"But I have always wanted to go to Burning Man," he added with a half-smile. "It's on my bucket list. The stories I've heard…."

"Me too!" I said. "It's supposed to be amazing."

As we parted again that morning, I knew it was possible that I would never see Finn again, but my stubborn heart didn't want to believe it.

Headstand at Royal Palace – Cambodia

Chapter 14

TORCHED

I was off again. Now that my year in Australia was cut to just three short months, my loose plan was to travel around Southeast Asia for six months. I was on what would end up as my "Teach, Pray, Love" tour, and Bali was first on the list.

Amanda came with me to Bali, where we spent our time trying to surf, visiting Komodo dragons, and lying on the beach listening to music with one earbud each. We also spent a few days in the Gili Islands, hanging at the beach bars.

One afternoon, we sampled a shroom shake and spent a hilarious couple of hours laughing and rolling in the shallow water until our skin was pruned and the high wore off. We met some people on the beach, made friends, and eventually went out to grab some pizza. Whenever I traveled with Amanda, it was an adventure. She had a knack for picking up strangers and turning them into friends.

Amanda and I stayed in Bali for two weeks, and it was just what I needed after the emotional upheaval of Australia. But it was over too quickly, and soon Amanda was on a flight back to New Jersey, and I was on my way to Cambodia.

In Cambodia, I met up with Carter. We taught English at an orphanage in Phnom Pen. It was eye-opening to live among the Cambodian people and to learn about the gruesome genocide that had ended only thirty years prior, resulting in the death of a quarter of its population. This meant everyone we encountered had been directly affected in some way. It was a harsh reality to confront. I had been to third-world countries and witnessed poverty before, but this was on another level.

Carter and I stayed at a hostel in Phnom Penh city. It was clean enough with air conditioning and a computer with free Wi-Fi downstairs. The orphanage where we taught was 20 minutes away, along rural back roads that were pitted and wound among stands of trees and homes built of concrete blocks with scaffolding and found materials. There were often animals rooting around the yards and rubbish thrown in the corners. Each morning, Carter and I would both jump on the back of a moto-taxi for the ride out, arriving dusty and disheveled to begin our day of teaching the kids.

The orphanage was a friendly place owned by a Dutch couple but run by an American guy my age who was married to a Cambodian woman. He cared deeply for the kids. Compared to other parts of Cambodia, the children here had opportunities. The orphanage not only cared for and educated them, but supported them through college if they wanted to go.

Despite the intense poverty, the people I met in Cambodia, particularly the children, were warm, positive and welcoming. My fondest memories were when we got to see the kids outside the classroom. Once we took them all to see *Frozen*. The cinema didn't have any seats so we all crammed on the floor together and they would not stop singing "Let it Go" for weeks after. Another time we all got invited to the wedding of an alumni student from the orphanage. I couldn't believe the extravagant Cambodian weddings, usually lasting three days. Everyone got dressed up and participated in traditional tea ceremonies, but when I looked past the glitz and glamour, all I could see was the joy on the kids' faces as they ran around in open spaces outside the chaotic city. The kids taught me how to be in the moment, appreciate the tiniest freedoms in life, and take nothing for granted.

Carter and I parted ways after five weeks—he headed to Singapore, and I headed to Vietnam—but we planned to meet back up in Myanmar. I arrived in the frenetic environment of Ho Chi Minh City and spent a few days seeing the sights. It wasn't really where I wanted to be, so after fighting the crowds of tourists, the throngs of locals, the motorbikes and cars, I decided to head up to the small coastal town of Nha Trang.

Nha Trang is a beach town, famous for its great winds and popular with kite surfers. Like most beach towns, the central part of the city sits on the esplanade along the beach. You would walk along the sidewalk, darting into the shade of overhanging awnings or scattered trees as much as possible to avoid the burning sun. The sea breeze didn't offer much relief from the humidity.

The main street had lots of little shops and stalls. Cho Hai seafood market with its myriad smells was underscored by a sharp salty tang that smelled more of the sea than the ocean itself. I enjoyed the ubiquitous American-style coffee shops, like

The Coffee House, where I would sit and sip Vietnamese coffee sweetened with heavy condensed milk and watch locals barter at the grocer across the road.

Mopeds bustled and whined everywhere just as they do in every town I'd visited in South East Asia. It didn't take long for the hums, roars and beeps to become the signature sound of my time there.

A moped driver also gave me my first sign of things to come.

∾

As soon as I arrived in Nha Trang, I hailed a moto-taxi for a ride to my hostel. A guy with longish hair pulled over and I hopped on the back of his blue moped. He sped off, me clinging to the back like a limpet. He took a right, then another right. Then after a minute, another right. This guy was taking me for a ride, physically and metaphorically.

When we finally got to the hostel, we were a mere two blocks from where I'd gotten on and he said it would be USD 10 for the ride, which I knew was way too much. But I hopped off and paid him, reserving my energies rather than engaging in a dispute. You win some you lose some…at least I knew I had a good sense of direction.

I shook it off, hauled my big red rucksack onto my shoulder, and walked through the hostel door. I took a deep breath of the salty air. I was just happy to be near a beach again. I always felt much better being close to a body of water.

The family-run hostel was in an alley just blocks off the beach. It was similar to so many others I had stayed in: a common area downstairs, a narrow, winding staircase with landings just large enough to turn around in, rooms with bunk beds and storage areas off of each landing, and one shared toilet (sometimes two if you're lucky).

It was cheap, cheerful, and filled with other travelers from around the world, all on their own journeys. As I headed up the stairs to my room on that first night, I passed by a couple hanging out wet clothes along the bed frame and laughing. I moved on quickly. The introvert in me didn't want to strike up a conversation.

The next morning, I sat alone finishing up the free omelet and toast for breakfast in the communal dining area. I stood and walked my plate over to the sink and then tossed my small knotted beach bag over my shoulder. I was dressed in my white bikini, a wrap, and flip-flops, heading out to spend the day on the beach.

I was just about out the door when the mom of the house poked her head out of the kitchen and said "Are you taking your wallet? Be careful. It might get stolen. Better to leave here." Her forehead wrinkled as she came to stand in front of me. She was tiny. All five feet of me towered over her.

I pulled my bag a little closer to me. I thought it was safer to keep it with me than to leave it in my room, but I didn't want to say that to her in case she was offended that I didn't think her home was safe. So, I just said, "Ah no that's all right. I'm good, thank you, though." Her face still showed concern, but I turned and made my way out of the hostel before she could say anything else, closing the door gently behind me.

It was early for me, not even 8 am, but it was already hot. The air was moist and I felt like I was walking through soup. I could feel myself sweating before I even made it the two blocks to the esplanade.

Once I got to the beach, I stepped onto the hot sand. There was a breeze coming in from the ocean, but it did nothing to alleviate the sun's fierce heat. There weren't many people on the beach because locals never went there for pleasure, and it was too windy for most people to enjoy a beach day. There were a few tourists on the beach, kite surfers out in the water, and locals fishing. I kept walking until I reached a very remote and empty part of the beach. I just wanted to be alone.

I spread out my thin travel towel and popped my earbuds in. Tropical house music came piping into my head. I laid back on the sand, my head bopping to the rhythm of the music, letting the sun go to work. I loved that feeling, the sun's rays heating my skin, soaking in all of that Vitamin D.

After a few minutes, I rolled over onto my stomach, dragging my iPhone with me. I spent a couple of minutes pushing the sand into a comfortable placement when I noticed a local guy squatting about ten feet away. He was sitting very still and rolling sand into balls.

I watched him for a few minutes from under my elbow, while I baked on the sand. Something seemed off, but he wasn't doing anything wrong. He was staring off into the ocean, not paying me any attention. Sweat was dripping from under my arm and down into my eyes as I watched him. I squeezed my eyes shut quickly, but the salty sweat made them burn. I sat up, deciding that I couldn't take the heat anymore. It was a matter of life or death. I needed to get into the water.

I stood up and tried brushing the sand off my belly, but I got nowhere as every grain was glued to my skin. I walked toward the ocean, backwards, keeping an eye on my belongings. The sun singed the skin on my shoulders. I had to get in and get cool.

I got to the water's edge and let out an audible sigh of relief as the cool water lapped against my ankles. I waded in up to my knees and just as I was about to lower myself in, aching for relief from the scorching heat, I saw the sand ball guy run straight for my towel.

I tried to stand, but it was as if I was moving in slow motion. I saw the water droplets catch the sunlight as they spun from my hands. But the sand ball guy seemed to be moving at warp speed. Before I could even step out of the water, he was at my towel, scooping up everything with both arms and clutching it to his chest, like you'd grab a runaway child. My towel, wallet, phone, keys, and even my sandals were held tight in his arms.

I lunged out of the water and started running after him. Even though I was wet the sand was already burning the soles of my feet, and every step felt like fighting quicksand.

I tried to scream, "Stop him! Stop him!" But it was like being stuck in a nightmare. No sound came from my throat. My voice was stuck. I dug in and tried to run faster, but I was let down by my adrenaline-fueled body which was quaking and shaking and abjectly failing to make up any ground. But I didn't stop. I couldn't. I kept running after him, screaming my voiceless screams.

He ran off the beach and onto the street. I knew what I looked like – a blonde-haired westerner, barefoot in a white bikini running hell for leather in the middle of a crowded city in Vietnam. I kept thinking that surely someone was going to stop him, but there he was ahead of me, dodging in and out of groups of people, shopping bags and kids under their arms, with no one doing a thing. As I continued my pathetic chase, I noticed the intentional blank looks of passersby. I wasn't getting any help. I lived in New York. I knew that look.

I wasn't sure how much longer I could keep it up when a black scooter lurched out of a side street and pulled up next to the thief. It didn't even stop as the thief jumped on the back, and they pulled away, disappearing along the boulevard's morning traffic. It was like a movie, and I realized then that it was all planned out. I was just another sucker tourist.

As they disappeared into the traffic, I watched my money; all of my access to money; and my connection to home, family, and friends disappear along with them. I put my hand on my chest. I could feel my heart pounding under my hand and I knew this was real, but I couldn't believe it, literally couldn't believe this was happening. It felt like a horrible dream. I was dead broke, half-naked, shoeless and desperate in a foreign country.

I bent over with my hands on my knees trying to catch my breath. I tried not to make eye contact with anyone. I was lost in my head, angry, alone, embarrassed and scared. I didn't know what else to do, so I just started walking back toward the hostel. I must have looked mad. I was talking to myself – no lecturing myself – about why I always seemed to end up in these situations. And why couldn't I just trust the woman at the hostel? And the whole time I was jumping from one shadow to the next trying to save my feet from the burning pavement.

I arrived back at the hostel in complete disarray, feet red and burnt and still sandy from the beach. My stomach was in knots. I was worried the owners would be upset. The key to my room was in that wallet. Then I realized, "Shit, I don't even have money to pay for the room." And I don't know how I'm going to get any money. All my cards were in that wallet and I have no way of getting one sent to me. Maybe they won't even let me stay.

I started talking to myself again, telling myself not to freak out, that everything was going to be OK. That somehow, it was going to work out, just like it always does.

Mercifully, the hostel owners were incredibly understanding. I was no doubt not the first naïve traveler for this to have happened.

"This is a big blessing," the woman who had warned me earlier said. "You'll see. Really big blessing." I found her and her husband in the kitchen again, doing the dishes. She was wearing an apron that was almost as long as she was tall, tied over faded blue shorts and a red patterned top. She smiled and patted my arm with her wet hands leaving a few drops of water rolling off onto the floor. Her husband, not much taller than her, lifted a Coca-Cola to his mouth. He let her get on with the talking.

"Thank you, I'm sure you're right," I said. But I didn't believe her. How could this be a blessing?

"We'll help you take care. Don't worry," she said. She nods toward the man. "Right?" she asked. He nodded, once, like a soldier given orders.

I nodded miserably in return. I wanted to sink on the floor of that hostel kitchen, bury my head in my hands and just cry. I wanted to give up and go home. But I also knew that was not an option. I still had two months to go before my return flight. I decided right then and there – in that tiny, overheated kitchen with kind strangers who were going to help me even though they had no obligation at all – that I was going to make this work, no matter what I had to do. I would not go home early.

The owners allowed me to use their laptop to email Dad. I organized for him to wire USD 200 to a Western Union as I cancelled all my cards. There was no possible way for me to get new cards physically, so when the new cards arrived at Dad's, he sent me the numbers to book flights and accommodations online. Not having any access to cash or cards until I met up with Carter meant I had to be crafty because most things were still cash only.

My appetite had been suppressed after being in fight or flight mode, but that night people at the hostel were throwing a rooftop BBQ that cost a few dollars to join. I swallowed my pride and asked them if I could come along even though I had nothing to contribute. They were more than happy to help and I was grateful. In my experience, people are kind, especially when you allow yourself to be vulnerable enough to ask for help.

The following day the hostel owner's son drove me to the Western Union on his scooter to make sure I received the money safely. Once I had that in my pocket, I felt much better although I knew it wasn't going to last long. I had to spend less.

My flight out of Vietnam was already booked to Bangkok and I had heard from other travelers that Thailand was one of the more expensive countries in Southeast Asia. This was concerning because I planned to be there for three weeks before my flight to Myanmar. Instead of freaking out, I put my resourceful pants on and turned to Google.

I sat at an internet café sipping an iced Vietnamese coffee, clicking on offers to volunteer with elephants and turtles or to teach English, but the programs' intake dates didn't overlap with my time frame. Feeling more and more frustrated, I kept searching before I stumbled on a week-long "donation-based" silent meditation retreat, in Ko Samui, Thailand. The retreat began a few days after the Full Moon Party I planned to go to in Ko Pha Ngan. The irony of dancing under the stars with thousands of people while looking forward to a week of silent, solitary contemplation pleased me. I applied and was accepted a few days later.

I didn't think much about the meditation part of the retreat, all I thought about was the money I would be saving. I didn't go in with the best intentions, yet my stay in Ko Samui would turn out to be the blessing foretold by the hostel owner. It would change my life forever, and I now know with great conviction that the incident on the beach was a moment of grace and that sand ball guy might as well have been an angel.

4:00 am	Morning wake-up bell
4:30 - 6:30 am	Meditate hall/ room
6:30 - 8:00 am	Breakfast break
8:00 - 9:00 am	Group meditation in hall
9:00 - 11:00 am	Meditate hall/ room
11:00 - 12:00 pm	Lunch Break
12:00 - 1:00 pm	Rest / Interviews
1:00 - 2:30 pm	Meditate hall/ room
2:30 - 3:30 pm	Group meditation in hall
3:30 - 5:00 pm	Meditate hall/ room
5:00 - 6:00 pm	Tea Break
6:00 - 7:00 pm	Group meditation in hall
7:00 - 8:15 pm	Discourse in the hall
8:15 - 9:00 pm	Group meditation in hall
9:00 - 9:30 pm	Question time in hall
9:30 pm	Lights out

Schedule for 10-day Vipassana Retreat

Chapter 15

HAZARD REDUCTION

The silent retreat was for meditation only and involved working. It was nothing like what you would expect from a typical wellness retreat – there were no massages or afternoon cocktails. There was no pool or beach to relax at or fancy meals and midday naps. But in one way, this retreat was like a fancy and costly retreat designed to reset the stressed-out traveler in that the property was gorgeous and one felt immediate calm on arrival.

I had been reading shelf-help, Buddhist and Zen books for over a decade at this point. The books helped me make sense of the world and find an anchor. Buddhist philosophy was how I built my strong muscles of faith and spirituality. All the books I read were about cultivating a mindset open to everything and attached to nothing. The books often mentioned both meditation and mindfulness as a way to develop an open, unattached mindset, but I didn't practice. Little did I know just how intoxicating meditation and mindfulness would be for me.

The buildings of the retreat sat on top of a steep mountain looking out toward the ocean. There were bright green lawns with long, straight pathways lined with orange flowers. Statuary adorned the palm tree-filled gardens, and in the mornings, you could sit under the open-air pagodas and watch the sunrise over the ocean. It was pure peace.

The sleeping quarters were basic. Being in a dorm with 13 other women didn't bother me. I grew up with four siblings and many cousins so we were always sharing beds, plus I'd been sleeping in hostels with plenty of strangers over the last few months.

There was minimal privacy and no place to store personal items. The bed was a flat elevated wooden base with no bedding and slabs of plywood acting as walls around it. I believe this was to eliminate distractions. The bed was equipped with a small piece of timber with a notch or u-shape to it, which I assumed was my pillow. I grew to love my makeshift shelter; it was soon my sanctuary.

When I arrived, most of the others were busy tucking sheets around the wooden frame or laying out blankets. I wasn't prepared and missed the memo to bring your own bedding. I was lucky I had a travel towel, sarong and a mosquito net hung above my bed. The showers were located below the sleeping quarters in a dark, dingy basement with no hot water. Me and cold don't mix, so I spent little time down there.

The rest of the spaces were all open. There were no closed rooms. The eating area had long tables where they'd place big bowls of oatmeal and fruit in the mornings and stir-fries for lunch. We were offered one piece of fruit and a cup of tea for dinner. Everything was self-serve, vegetarian and simple, yet it was all so delicious. Maybe it was because you didn't have a choice and those were the only two meals you had each day. Whatever the reason, I always enjoyed the food.

The meditation areas were simple spaces with a roof but no windows, open to nature. A single wall in the front of the room had a Buddha and poster of The Noble Eightfold Path. The Noble Eightfold Path summarizes eight Buddhist practices that lead to enlightenment through ethical conduct, mental discipline and wisdom. That's what we were there to study. Strewn across the room were pillows to sit on for meditation and to help you find comfort. For those not comfortable sitting on the ground, chairs were available.

At first, the 4 am wake-up calls and meditations were tough. The day and austerity settings proved a challenge, but having a regimented schedule gave me a daily sense of purpose and direction.

And there was no social anxiety for there was no getting to know the other participants. This was a silent retreat. We weren't allowed to talk at any point and were instructed not to make eye contact with anybody. Everyone studiously followed these rules and avoided any contact. In the evenings, you were allowed to line up to ask the facilitator questions but I never had any questions. The process and concepts were straightforward. The practices were rigid both physically and mentally, but easy to follow.

Not speaking was my favorite element of the retreat. When you are backpacking, you get asked the same questions over and over. I'm not a fan of small talk at the best of times; being silent felt like a relief. I didn't have to present myself to anyone in any way. I didn't owe anything to anyone. I could just be in the moment, exploring myself – my humanity.

It was the polar opposite of the life I'd just left, yet I quickly adapted to a monk's life. The Buddha's teachings clicked for me. I loved the simplicity, the routine, the pace and the fact that I didn't have to make any decisions or do anything but devote myself to my meditations. I could feel my body moving into a relaxed state. I realized that I could read all the books and listen to all the advice, but if I didn't physically put my body in the appropriate environment, it would never be able to heal fully.

Every morning, we would be awoken in the complete dark by the chime of a bell. We'd have 15 minutes to dress, brush our teeth, walk up the hill stairs to the meditation hall and find our place for our first meditation of the day. It was always lit with candles and there was always incense burning. I loved the ambience. At first, I'd pull heaps of pillows around me, supporting my knees and butt. I was careful not to face the soles of my feet toward the teachers or the Buddha statue (a sign of disrespect). But over the days, I found I needed the pillows less and less, as I became more practiced at sitting.

We spent about six hours a day meditating. The meditations were broken up into thirty-minute sessions throughout the day, and we had the option to do walking meditations for some of the sessions. Walking meditations involved walking in a small area at a languid and methodical pace; I found them more brutal than sitting. I'd find myself having to work hard not to stroll at speed and take in the sights like I was on a scenic hiking tour. Naturally, I am fast walker and there was nothing more annoying to a New Yorker than sauntering.

In the afternoons, we would have Dhamma talks where we would learn about the teachings of the Buddha. As I sat and listened over the days that followed, it was like the world started to come into focus. I had read and resonated with these teachings for over a decade but all the information in my brain I had accumulated from books started to make more sense now in my body. I was experiencing the teachings deeply through mindfulness meditations.

Intellectualizing Buddha's teachings only got me to a certain point. Meditation was the key to grasping them. Understanding comes through experience and trying to comprehend the Buddha's teaching by just reading books is like trying to understand what wet feels like by reading the word water.

The teachings of the Buddha are extremely simple, but that doesn't mean they are easy to practice. They are about understanding the true nature of reality and seeing things for how they are, not how you wish them to be. Unfortunately, we are constantly disconnected from this because we spend so much time seeking desired experiences while harboring an aversion to unpleasant ones. We don't naturally allow experiences to come without craving some and avoiding others.

Meditation was helping me learn how to walk this noble path. I started replacing my "either-or" thinking with "both-and." Accepting what is but also working on changing what is. Sitting there for all those hours instilled a new way of *being* into me. I became more patient, open, humble and curious about the stuff that was coming up. Instead of reacting, I was observing. I was starting to have more compassion for my often-scattered mind and the cycles I found myself stuck in. I was finding more meaning and understood life more clearly.

I wouldn't say that I like secrets, so a philosophy that holds truth as its highest value is one that I can get behind. Buddhist philosophy is a science that says: suffering exists, it has a cause, it has an end and it has a cause to bring about its end. The Buddha believed that our suffering exists because of attachments and the cause to bring about its end, is to simply let go of attachments or in his wise words, "you can only lose what you cling to."

We don't wake up every day with a movie script that tells us precisely what will happen. We are all just rowing our own boats gently down the stream. The more we row the more we let go. The more we let go the better we feel. *Merrily merrily merrily merrily, life is but a dream.*

At the silent retreat I was introduced to yoga as a pathway to meditation. I'd tried yoga once or twice in college as a form of working out but didn't like it. This retreat was more about mindful movements. It felt boring but good to do something other than meditation. Every morning before lunch, we had a yoga class taught by a woman in her 60s who also participated in the retreat. It was impressive to watch her be the most flexible person in the room as well as the most cheerful. I wondered if it was yoga that kept her like this.

The days went on – each day like the last, hardly changing. But I was changing. During meditations, my mind was sharper. I could sit longer and I was learning to stretch both my body and my mind during yoga. Each day I'd wake up feeling just a little bit different – a little more grounded, a little less driven by chance and a little more connected to nature – the plants, the swaying palm trees and even the annoying flies.

I assumed that perhaps I had much less to think or stress about compared to most people there as I had every single belonging that I owned with me. I had no children, animals, job, house, car, relationship or any asset waiting for me back home (except for a student loan). I didn't even have a phone, so the only messages I ever got were emails from a friend or family member. I saw this as a great benefit, as fewer distractions meant better concentration.

I might wonder how I should be grieving for my mom or what I should do with my life after Asia. Yet soon the thoughts became meaningless worries when they arrived in meditations. The point was simple – notice when the mind wandered and gently, with compassion (if possible), bring it back to focusing on the breath. In and out. Over and over. That's all. There was absolutely nothing to believe in but everything to discover.

Having the patience and tenacity to keep bringing my awareness back to my breath allowed me to understand how worrying about my past or future wouldn't change the outcome. Instead, it would only change my experience in that present moment. One thing had already happened, my mom passed away. I couldn't change it. And the other, what I will do when I leave Asia, was so far in the future that I had no idea what could happen by then. The only moment I had was right now—this breath.

A shift that shocked me was how my stomach issues miraculously disappeared but only for that week. I doubt it was from the oatmeal and rice but how could my brain have such a direct influence over my gut? All the doctors and specialists I went to never mentioned anything about meditating. Their advice was to go on a Low Fodmap (sugar-restrictive) Diet or to just accept that I may never be "regular."

During one of the talks, the teacher shared an analogy. "Thoughts are like birds. You can't keep them from flying around your head, but you can keep them from building nests in your hair." I had never realized how much control I had over my thoughts, feelings and emotions. I found this intensely liberating and I breathed in that new sense of freedom a little more each day.

The human attention span is short, so practicing mindfulness—the art of living in the present moment—is essential. A straightforward challenge showed how difficult it is to live in each second: On the first day, the teacher asked us to count how many scoops it took to finish our breakfast. On the last day, he asked us if anyone could recall how many mouthfuls it took to finish a morning's breakfast. Not one of us could raise our hands. I had attempted to keep track a few times. I'd start off excited, "1, 2, 3, ugh this is so boring, this is pointless, I don't need to do this. I'll try it tomorrow." The next day, "1, 2, 3, 4, 5, 6,...12. Look at me, this is easy. I'm totally going to get this. 13, 14. Look at that butterfly. I can't believe that person is going back for thirds. Did the facilitator say that was allowed? Maybe I'll go back for more today." I could never get to the end of my meal before distracting thoughts took over. Neither could anybody else, and that's just how the brain works. We are constantly venturing into the past or future, only rarely do we stay in the present moment. Mindfulness is a muscle; through practice, we can slowly increase our attention to the present moment.

A big take-home from the retreat I still practice daily is the metta meditation. Metta is a Pali language word for loving-kindness and during this type of meditation, we would learn how to send positive energy and kindness toward others. The teacher said that all beings on this planet want to live in peace and that nobody or nothing is more deserving or less deserving of safety, health and happiness so we would learn how to spread this message in our meditation.

Before we began, he explained that to give loving-kindness we must first and foremost cultivate loving-kindness within ourselves. You can only give what you have.

His trick to cultivating a feeling of loving-kindness was to envision a baby or puppy and to focus on their face. Imagine looking into their eyes, noticing how they don't judge and accept everyone just as they are. This is the essence of loving-kindness—a place where curiosity, joy and unconditional love can only exist.

With this powerful feeling, you then visualize a picture of yourself and repeat the following phrases silently to yourself. "May you be safe. May you be healthy. May you be happy. May you live in peace." Repeat the phrases for a few moments over and over, letting the warm unconditional love feeling sink in. After that, you take someone you respect, maybe a parent or a teacher, and say the same thing to them.

Next, visualize someone you love and imagine saying the same thing to them, taking in that loving-kindness feeling. Fourth, imagine a neutral person. This is someone you have no emotional attachment to or may not know. Repeat the statements.

Fifth, visualizing someone you dislike, fear or find challenging, is the hardest. It could be a person or thing. I didn't use a person at the time but I used cockroaches because I couldn't think of anything more repulsive. Last but certainly not least, visualize the entire planet, all the people, animals, nature, and sentient beings and wish the same for everything. Spread your loving-kindness to every part of the world.

While learning this type of meditation and reflecting on my childhood, I realized that I had been doing this for as long as I could remember. When I was very young, I would lie in bed before falling asleep and say the "Lord's prayer" which is the only thing I could recollect from my Catholic upbringing. After that, I would ask God to watch over me, all my family and friends so we would all be happy, healthy and safe. I would visualize as many faces as possible and if I knew someone who needed an extra bit of help, I would specifically say their name.

The only religious thing we did while growing up was midnight mass and my parents never talked to us about God, yet I prayed every night. I didn't know with whom I was speaking, but I always maintained a connection to my spiritual side. There was a period when I stopped praying because I felt like an imposter talking to something I didn't understand.

Finally, through metta meditation, I found a way to have that communication again without needing to understand the word 'God'. I could simply just wish the best for people, including myself. It felt good to deliberately focus on sending out good intentions again.

Each day passed, like a separate world of its own. I did the work. I meditated, ate, listened to the talks, practiced yoga, and slept. Then did it all again the next day. But within those limited activities, something inside was blossoming and growing. I wasn't speaking to anyone; I was listening to myself. I was finally listening to the Katie that had always been there. Her spirit felt familiar, yet her voice had been hidden from me for some time. I had put up walls to protect her. I saw how I had fallen into unhealthy habits and routines that didn't serve my best self. Patterns that didn't make me feel like a great person the next day, only fueled my anxieties.

I felt inspired to live a new path. One that was closer to The Noble Eightfold path. I wanted to do things that would consciously help alleviate my suffering instead of enhancing it. I was never going to become 100% perfect, but at least now I had a practical method through meditation to put my efforts into practice.

We gathered in the communal area on the last day to fill in our donation envelopes. People spoke quietly among themselves, gathering their belongings to head home. I filled my envelope out and surreptitiously snuck in only a few colorful Thai bills. As I handed it over, I felt self-conscious because my situation meant I wasn't able to donate much money. I felt indebted to a place that ultimately changed the trajectory of my life.

I enjoyed the minimalistic lifestyle and living with fewer attachments that week. I loved wearing the same five outfits of shapeless cotton pants and loose-fitting shirts with no accessories and no heels. Even though I looked like the old Katie, I knew I would never be her again. I was a human being no longer a human doing. I liked my new version.

Taking in the Buddha's energy - Myanmar

Photo by: Colin Lieu

Chapter 16

SPARK

After the retreat, I met up with Carter in Myanmar where my connection to Buddhism deepened. The big Buddha statues everywhere calmed my nervous system.

Myanmar hadn't been open long to tourists, so we were a novelty. For a country that had seen a lot of turmoil, the people went above and beyond in their hospitality. They looked you in the eye when they were talking; I felt the teachings of the Buddha flow through its people.

Carter and I travelled the roads of Myanmar on rented bikes. We spent days exploring a country where nine out of ten people were Buddhist. We travelled circuitous routes along roads that hugged the steep sides of mountains to reach stunning and deserted pagodas. We'd spend an hour or two wandering, feeling the connections and meditating. All of the places we visited felt untouched.

In Myanmar, it was illegal for foreigners to ride mopeds in every city except one, Mandalay. It was here that I learned to ride a moped for the first time and was pulled over by the police. They didn't speak any English and I didn't speak any Burmese nor did I have a license. It ended with a bunch of shoulder shrugs and laughs, no bribery and I think they just wanted to say hello to some Westerners.

Later that day, I succumbed to a stomach bug and remembered the deep-fried dough that caught my eye from the street vendor outside our hostel. It looked and tasted delicious, but something wasn't right. My stomach began to churn after the police let us go. I didn't want to lose the day, so I held on tight, hoping it would pass.

It didn't pass.

We puttered onto the grounds of a humble and beautiful pagoda. I parked the moped and we started climbing the stairs to its tiered peak. We got about halfway and it hit me. It was horrific. The kind of thing you hear about from other stories but hope never to experience yourself.

I was fortunate it wasn't a major tourist attraction. Otherwise, this would have been some predicament. There were no trees, no toilets and not even any grass, just a bunch of dried-up bush leaves. There was nothing I could do, I had to let it all come out on top of a mountain in Myanmar. Once I was able to get up, I staggered over to the nearest bench and didn't move for an hour as my stomach did backflips.

To this day I can recall laying on that bench, thinking how physically awful I felt but at the same time how mentally peaceful. I was content to be there despite the thrashing going on inside. Dealing with pain through understanding impermanence is the essence of Buddhist philosophy. I knew the pain would eventually pass because nothing ever stays the same. I was truly living in the moment. Experiencing life without clinging desperately to my own comfort, avoiding the pain or wishing for it to be different.

I started to replace my anxiety with gratitude. I was grateful for being brave that morning, learning how to ride a moped in a hectic city, for the cops being so lovely and letting us go, and for arriving safely at the pagoda without getting lost. Above all, I was grateful for the simple fact that nobody was around and that I had a friend who was happy to wait patiently while my dreadful pain passed.

Reflecting on that moment, the only difference was a shift in perspective. I had the power to accept myself exactly where I was and focus on reality. I didn't lie there in misery worrying about ifs, ands or buts. Lao Tzu, the author of the Tao Te Ching said, "When you accept yourself, the whole world accepts you." I was developing this new way of radical acceptance into my being.

I looked at the dried-up foliage, the temple, and the mountain itself and opened my heart. I let myself be present with where I was right at that moment. I finally knew that I didn't need to be anything, anywhere and I certainly didn't need to search for something that was missing. Everything that I had learned throughout my life and the recent experiences at the retreat were coalescing and reaffirming in my mind. I had everything that I needed inside of me.

∼

But it wasn't as easy to reach states of deep meditation outside of a meditation retreat. I missed the introspection and stable routine I'd found. So, when me and Carter parted ways, I went back to the internet. This time I narrowed my Google search to "donation-based silent meditation retreats" and came across Vipassana centers that run all over the world on donations. Vipassana is a type of meditation that means insight. I found a center in Malaysia, with a program that would end a few days before my flight home. Newcomers were required to do a 10-day silent retreat and I had just finished a seven-day silent retreat. What're three extra days?

The common areas at the Malaysia center were set up similar to Thailand and just as serene. It was also a welcome relief to see the living quarters were private rooms with bathrooms rather than communal ones.

Though the premises were more comfortable, the meditations were more intense. Each meditation lasted 1 to 3 hours, roughly 10 hours a day. You were not allowed to talk, read, write or exercise – including yoga. Again, only two small vegetarian meals before noon. And there was a one-hour video discourse at the end of each day to explain the Vipassana technique, how it works and how to integrate it into your daily life.

Unlike the last retreat, fewer travelers and more locals were in attendance. In Thailand, you could sit anywhere you wanted for meditation but you are given designated seats at Vipassana retreats. Other than in the meditation hall, men and women are kept separate. The goal was to maintain the least number of distractions so you could do brain surgery without a scalpel.

There was one male and one female assistant teacher and neither spoke. They silently meditated in the hall facing the students to ensure we followed the rules. That was the only time I saw them, and there were only two times in the day to ask them questions regarding the technique – at lunch and before bed. They made me uncomfortable. It felt like they were watching, judging and waiting for someone to meditate the wrong way.

All the teachings were conducted through recordings broadcasted over speakers. They featured Satya Narayan Goenka, a man from Myanmar who carried the Vipassana method to India in 1969, which then filtered worldwide.

Even though the audio recordings and videos were old and clunky, the teachings felt so much more authentic through the crackling and echoing of voices. It gave a sense that this had been listened to thousands of times and that I was a part of an age-old tradition. There wasn't anything to try and understand, you just had to be present and observe. When your mind drifted, you would bring your attention back to the body or breath. With such a narrow focus, it wasn't easy to sit still for such long periods, and I didn't enjoy it for the most part. It was hard and I couldn't help but question why it felt like torture.

I constantly compared myself to the people around me who were statue-like, downright motionless for hours. I wasn't sure I could ever achieve such stillness. Throughout the day they had three "sittings of determination" where it was encouraged to pause and not move for the entire hour of meditation. The mind can be your own worst enemy regarding the "sittings of determination." When the pressure of no movement is on, it becomes harder to relax and let go. At least for myself, when these "sittings of determination" were not declared, I found it much easier to sit in meditations without flinching.

I trusted the method and did the work to the best of my ability. Truthfully, I slept through the sessions where you were allowed to meditate in your room. Maybe that's why the other retreat didn't have mattresses or private rooms. Despite my failings, my internal shift in mindset was clear and undeniable. The process *was* working and I knew my old ways were done. New York City was out of the question. I couldn't go back to a city full of temptations and wildly unhealthy ways.

The ten days passed in much the same way the previous 7-day retreat had. The days repeated themselves full of stillness and self-exploration.

When the meditation retreat ended, the changes it made in me continued. As I boarded the plane to return to America, I saw the world through different eyes. I looked around the airplane and felt genuinely connected to the people around me. I felt like our energies and essences combined and interacted beautifully and inevitably like one big ball of synchronicity.

Chapter 17

SAME FLAME

I had a short layover in Los Angeles to catch up with a friend. Emily and I had worked together in New York City and since she moved, she'd rave about how much she loved the lifestyle of LA. I wanted a change in scenery. The weather, plus what seemed like a healthier way of life, aligned with my new self.

I didn't know exactly how I would make the transition across the country work with no job or place to live, but the universe must have heard me because while I was there, Emily introduced me to some friends who needed a new housemate. It's uncanny how when something is meant for you, the world will conspire to help you get there.

The townhouse was a low-set brick building on a quiet, tree-lined street four blocks from the beach on the cusp of Santa Monica and Venice in Ocean Park. It was a short walk to Main Street, Rose Avenue, Abbot Kinney, Lincoln Boulevard and the 3rd street promenade. There wasn't much action going on in the streets and it was way more suburban than New York City. That is exactly what I was after.

I knocked, and when the door opened, a girl my age stood there. She was tiny in every way except for her big brown eyes and white smile complemented by perfect pink lipstick. She introduced herself as Val and invited me in. Emily told me that Val had just started working for a brand-new meditation app called Headspace. It was hard not to geek out on Val because of my new found obsession with meditation, I was secretly impressed.

The enormous living room had three couches, perfect for a share house. You could do multiple cartwheels on the area rug without hitting anything, and that was just part of the first floor. As we travelled up the staircase, I was gobsmacked that it was two stories with four bedrooms and three bathrooms plus a living, dining and kitchen area. I was there to check out Val's bedroom, where I would be sharing a bathroom with Liv, who lived across the hall.

Liv came out to say hi. She was friendly, talking about going to a USC football game and how excited she was for the season to start. She loved sports of all kinds and later I found out that she worked for a well-known health brand. I thought, does everyone have awesome jobs?

Liv, Val and I were standing around talking about my travels and what brought me out to LA, when we heard Raquel, the other roommate who lived downstairs, come through the door. She yelled out, "Heeeey everybody, where are you!?"

Liv yelled back, "Upstairs. Katie's here. We'll come down to you." We all marched down the carpeted stairs and sat on different couches, just because we could. Raquel immediately plopped on the ground and started foam rolling as we chatted about what brought me out to LA.

Then Raquel mentioned working for a non-profit organization that hosted grassroots events. So, everyone in LA had hip jobs.

"It's been great to meet you," Raquel said, still foam rolling, a big grin on her face. Liv nodded behind her, and Val echoed with her own, "Yeah."

"We have to interview one more person tomorrow" Liv added. "But I'll let you know soon."

I nodded. "Sure," I said. "No problem." We chatted for a bit longer and then I left with confidence as the door shut behind me. Something inside of me *knew* I was going to live there.

When I flew back to West Virginia, I saw it through new eyes. The trees were greener, the light brighter and even the freshly cut grass smell was better. For the first time, I didn't take it for granted or think it was boring but I appreciated its untouched nature.

It was odd going back to the house where I'd spent my irritable adolescent years and life-changing last days with my mom. Now, it was Dad's house. Strangely, he had slotted into her life just as she'd always wanted him to.

I loved seeing my dad again, telling him about my travels, all I'd learned and how I had changed. However, West Virginia didn't hold much for me. I was beginning to feel restless, contemplating my next move when fate stepped in. Liv wrote to me saying that while the room I'd looked at wasn't available anymore, another roommate had decided to move out so if I was still interested, I had a place in California.

Once again, I was granted a humble reminder that life is full of great surprises and wonderful coincidences. The new room was four times the size of my bedroom in New York City with a walk-in closet and a bathroom. I took it!

I packed up my two bags again – everything I owned – kissed my dad goodbye, and drove 2,366 miles in my mom's white Volvo. I called it the white whale because of its ghastly turning radius. My mom loved that car and as I drove down the highway toward California, I had her support holding me tight.

When I pulled up in front of the apartment building in the white whale, I was greeted by the friendly guy who lived nearby. He was leaving his house when I passed him with an arm full of clothes slipping off their hangers. I hadn't bothered to pack them into suitcases. I figured it was much easier to transport closet to closet.

He came to the car, in shorts and a t-shirt and said, "Volvo, very safe. Hi, I'm Thomas, Liv said you were arriving today." He had an English accent and a welcoming smile.

"Hey, I'm Katie," I said as I reached around to pop the trunk.

"Let me help you get your stuff inside," Thomas said. He walked around and lifted the trunk up.

"It's not much," I said, laughing. But he just nodded and began pulling bags out. So, I grabbed the small things in the backseat and followed him up the path. Something like this would never happen in New York, I thought. I got a parking spot right out front, and a random neighbor is helping me move. More confirmation vibes that LA was the right path.

Thomas helped me deposit the stuff into my room. Then he showed me where he lived two doors down and told me to let him know if I needed help finding anything.

"I'm headed to work now," Thomas said. "But I'm sure I'll see you around."

"Definitely," I said, "and thank you." He nodded again and left through the front door, leaving it wide open behind him.

I thought that was a little strange but it turned out, that's how California people live.

Living in the townhouse was like being back in college. I had three roommates of course, but the neighbors, including Thomas, were like our second and third set of roommates. It was so casual that we would leave the doors open and walk into each other's apartments whenever the mood took us.

The LA lifestyle was very different from New York in other ways, too. Instead of sipping on Bellinis and Bloody Marys at a Sunday brunch, we would go for a sunrise hike followed by green smoothies. Living four blocks from the beach meant every evening there was a magnificent Pacific sunset to enjoy; I was there every day. My endless application process for marketing jobs had yet to yield a job, so I found some nanny work in the meantime.

A month into being there, I was accepted as a test pilot for a new fitness program. I was excited about the opportunity because I assumed I would get in the best shape of my life. You know what they say when you *ass-u-me*?

The program consisted of three meals and two snacks plus a workout regime for 90 days. I even had to take the awkward bikini "before" photo. I really felt like a local now.

I ate a clean diet of high protein, nuts, seeds, fruits and veggies, worked out and didn't drink alcohol. Only water, plain tea or coffee was allowed. And because I could only eat the food given to me, I wasn't going out for dinners or on dates. I was mostly spending my free time meditating in my closet. It was the best place to get away from all the noise.

This also meant I wasn't meeting new people, but I didn't mind having all that alone time. It was a complete shift from being a bar-hopping social butterfly in New York City to a sensible meditating monk in Los Angeles. I loved it. I discovered that I'd always desired an excuse to make a healthier choice and embrace my inner hermit.

The program finished up just before Christmas and let's just say, it wasn't a huge success. One of the producers saw that I wasn't getting results a few weeks prior and suggested I replace meals with shakes. That didn't happen.

I ended up only losing 3 lbs. and gaining muscle mass. My clothes fit tighter and I didn't *feel* any better. To top it off, it was shaping up to be a lonely Christmas while my housemates were off with their families. So, when my friend Megan messaged saying she was flying in from Australia, I invited her to stay. It was nice to have a friendly face to catch up with and of course, when it came down to having a few drinks, I caved. Those few drinks turned into many. Old habits die hard.

I hadn't drunk like that in over a year so with no tolerance built up, I got completely and utterly wasted. It was so bad that at one point I fell flat on my face on the dance floor and later that night we were kicked out of a guy's apartment because I was being rude.

When we finally ended up stumbling home, I couldn't get my keys to work. There was nothing wrong with the key and there was nothing wrong with the lock, but we just couldn't make it work.

I stood on Megan's shoulders to break through the window instead. Megan was standing in heels on a staircase while I climbed over her and bashed through the window screen. Little did we know one of the roommates was home that night. Thankfully, it was only the screen I had to replace.

The next morning was awful, and I'm not talking about the pounding headache and upset stomach. I was filled with regret. I was in Shame Shack on Struggle Street, berating myself over and over for the dumb things I'd done. My old relationship with alcohol wasn't conducive to my new relationship with wellness.

Megan left and I was alone for a few days to wallow in my self-pity. I avoided everything Christmassy and spent the days meditating and hanging around on the beach, even though it was much too cold to swim. I'd sit on the icy sand with a book or a notebook watching the waves crash on the shore. The sun was shining but it still felt dreary and dismal; however, an unexpected e-gift came on Christmas Eve.

A season's greetings email from Finn. He was a dutiful person, so the fact that he'd sent a Merry Christmas and Happy New Year message didn't surprise me. What caught me off guard was that he said he missed me and that I was always on his mind and in his heart. I read that part several times over, luxuriating in the sensation of the words sinking in. Always on his mind. Always in his heart.

After I'd read it for the sixth time and was certain I wasn't reading wrong, I pushed back from the computer and stared out the window. What did this mean? He was still with his fiancé, wasn't he? Just like always, I was thrilled to hear from him. He was always on my mind, too. But, just like always, this message left me confused.

My fingers hovered over the keyboard because I wanted to reply but I wasn't sure what to say. Why was I still holding on? And what was I holding onto? I casually replied the next day, knowing it would go nowhere and I shouldn't get my hopes up.

Karma yogi at the ashram - Caribbean

Chapter 18

BURNING OFF

After New Year's, I started to get an itch. The type of cool job everybody else had never come through for me, despite sending out resumes and exhausting every contact. I didn't want to be a nanny forever and more than that, I didn't have the feeling that I'd found my new home.

I was living frugally, paycheck to paycheck, and the friendships I made never seemed to stick. My roommates were great, but they were never home. Maybe I wasn't cool enough, pretty enough, or rich enough in LA. Or perhaps I didn't have the right connections or the right jobs.

My initial response when something doesn't feel right is to leave, but I didn't have the financial freedom. So, my wanderlust mind started to think about volunteering again, but where? I remembered a girl I met travelling, telling us about an Ashram in the Caribbean where you could do karma yoga. Karma yoga is selfless service or action performed for the benefit of others – without expecting anything in return.

I googled it and the first link was a yoga retreat on an island in paradise. I clicked on the drop-down menu on ways to visit and there it was – Apply for Karma Yoga Program and the next intake date was my 29th birthday, my Saturn's return. In astrology, when Saturn returns to your birth sign (every 27-29 years) one can expect a year of significant change and learning.

There were only a few requirements to be accepted into the karma yoga program. The first was that you had to stay for at least three months. The second was that you had to work in a role that would assist the ashram. And third, you had to live in a tent. All of this felt easy enough for me. Once I was accepted into the program, all I had to do was find someone my roommates approved to take my room. A few days later a roommate's friend got in touch as he was moving to LA and needed a temporary place. Not only that but he let me borrow his tent. There goes the universe scheming to help me again…I was off to the Caribbean!

∼

The Caribbean was idyllic—white sand beaches with crystal-clear blue water and pink skies. The only way on and off the Island was by boat from the mainland. The only other infrastructure on the Island was the biggest, most commercial hotel and casino in the Caribbean. Such dualities.

Living at the ashram was no different from living in any other small community. There were personalities and politics, gossip and drama, and even though you were supposed to abstain from all sexual activity, it was going on. Not for me, but it was hard to hide when we all lived in tents. You were also meant to abstain from alcohol and caffeine, but I heard of people going to the hotel and Starbucks.

Then there were your "saint makers," those people with unfriendly personality traits or who were not easy to work with. Life is cruisy when people are friendly but it takes real work to have compassion toward rude or inconsiderate behavior, hence their name...saint makers.

There was other drama and because I worked the front desk, I saw a lot of it, but one incident, in particular, I'll never forget. One day I was checking out a guest when he leaned over and asked me quietly if I would take his leftover magic mushrooms. He didn't want to take them back home through customs.

I said I'd take them but I had no plans to consume them, so I told some fellow Karma Yogis and a few had an awesome night-time beach session. Unfortunately, they all got kicked out a few weeks later. They assured me it wasn't my fault but I still felt responsible.

I had come to the Ashram to get away from parties and drug-taking. I had done a straight one-eighty. Any kind of stimulant was banned including onions, garlic and coffee. You were there to naturally detox. The most hardcore thing I did was eat chocolate and even that was rare! Other smaller dramas happened all the time as well. There was a communal laundry room and one time a guest's hip yoga tights went "missing." Another time, a Karma Yogi left in the middle of the night without telling anybody after only having spent a few days there.

In other ways, living in an ashram felt a lot like what I could only describe as a church camp even though I'd never been to one. The schedule was packed from sunup to sundown. From 5:30 – 7:30 am we were required to attend Satsung, where we sang, chanted, listened to talks or sermons, and performed cleansing connection rituals. Immediately after that, we had our regular staff meeting followed by breakfast and then we were off to work seven-hour shifts. You were also required to do at least one yoga class and another Satsung at night. The next day we'd wake up and do it all over again. There wasn't much downtime and no days off.

Unlike other staff, I was lucky enough to spend most of my day in air-conditioning. While on shift, I mingled with all the moving parts of the business and more importantly, I was responsible for the boat that got you on and off the island.

The ashram was not only a place for Karma Yogis. It was a hotel with paying customers who sometimes paid big bucks for a beachfront room. It was also a retreat center and place for students to get their Yoga Teacher Training certificates. The reception dealt with guests, Karma Yogis, cleaners, massage therapists, staff members, payments and registrations.

Even though I was immersed in a spiritual environment, my meditation practice was non-existent. I was used to meditating inside, in complete silence, with no distractions, so living in an outdoor retreat center with no buildings or private areas made it hard to find quiet time to be alone. Even in my tent or the temple you could always hear people walking around and talking.

Before the ashram, I still had only done yoga a handful of times and still, I despised it. I had a lot of resistance toward the obligatory daily two-hour yoga class. I preferred a class where I could sweat, stretch and lose my breath. I was still focused on losing weight and the warm homemade bread for breakfast didn't help that goal.

The worst part of the practice for me was the 20-minute breathing exercise (pranayama). I couldn't understand how anybody had lung capacity. The class was the same routine every single day with the same twelve poses in the same order with a savasana in between, which meant lying on your back doing nothing, at least ten times. I could never relax in savasana, it felt like an inane exercise.

My mentality at the time was that these silly yoga classes would never going to get me to my fitness goals. I figured I was already flexible and didn't need to stretch. What I really wanted was to lose that extra fifteen pounds, but at the ashram, I was doing work from the inside out instead of the outside in. I was now absorbing the philosophy of yoga and exposed to how the science of yoga works. I learned that yoga means to yoke or union with oneself and it was a way of life, not just a class you attend. It was more like a "work-in" rather than a "workout." A moving meditation.

Despite believing that yoga wasn't working for me, I was finding peace in other ways. Connecting and working with people in the community from all walks of life was helping me keep my mind and heart open. I saw how my attitude in New York City was toxic righteousness that had me full of cynicism and judgements. It left me not caring about the walls I built up, but being a yogi required me to learn and grow in a community dependent on one another. There was no room for distrust. This helped me knock down some of those walls. I guess I was doing yoga after all.

Life in the ashram meandered along, and I must admit, I enjoyed time away from the "real world." Even though I still had no answers about where I wanted to be, or what I wanted to do, it didn't seem to matter as much on the Island. Everyone else was a little lost or inhabiting an in-between phase. I could see how people would go there to escape a temporary reality, and end up staying for years. For me, it was always a stopover, not a stay.

Then, a year to the day from the morning I'd had all my things stolen on a beach in Vietnam, I received an email from Finn.

Before opening the email, I paused, looking at his name. What did I hope for? Did I secretly wish for a lifeline to pull me out of my tropical island paradise and back to whatever life had in store? If I had the choice to manifest my own destiny right now, what would it be?

I was too impatient to see what he had to say to spend time manifesting. I opened the email. There was a lot of text, but my eyes immediately snagged on five words midway down the page: *Sarah and I split up.*

My face split into a big grin. I was at the front desk and wasn't meant to be checking my emails, so I quickly forced a professional expression back onto my face.

The email ended hoping we could reconnect and still be friends.

Despite my excitement, I couldn't help feeling a flush of annoyance as well. What the hell does *"reconnect"* mean? But of course, that's what I had been waiting for all this time –my second chance with Finn.

As I thought about Finn, all the confusion and unrest about where my life was going subsided, just for a second. The gates of the exciting unknown had just reopened for business.

I immediately replied this time with fresh hope and kept our email exchange going, but I certainly wasn't going to skip back to Australia anytime soon. I was focused on myself and committed to finishing up my time at the ashram.

∼

My 3-month compulsory stay at the ashram ended as the rainy season began. One night I woke to a giant cockroach crawling up my leg. Then the rains began and tents flooded. It was time for me to move on.

I decided to volunteer at the Kid's Yoga Camp run by the same ashram. I would still live in a tent but this time in the cooler Canadian woods. I hadn't worn makeup in months and shaving was no longer a thing so my rugged look lived on. Since the ashram had the same dress code as the meditation retreats in Asia, knees and shoulders covered at all times, my wardrobe consisted of the same five pairs of loose cotton pants and baggy T-shirts. I borrowed boots that were two sizes too big for me from a fellow karma yogi since I was working in the kitchen, I needed to keep my feet safe.

The schedule was similar to the Caribbean, but it was Canada so all the buildings were enclosed. I began practicing meditation more regularly, using the mantra given to me when I was initiated into the tradition. I kept to myself to avoid forming any close friendships, but at the kids' final performance I was in tears, questioning how my life might have been any different if I'd come to a summer camp based on yoga and meditation as a child. Watching the kids enjoy yoga and meditation in a fun and digestible way gave me faith in the next generation.

∼

After a month at the Kid's Camp, I travelled back down to New York City to visit Amanda, who was now living with Carter in Brooklyn.

While lying in Amanda's bed scrolling Facebook, I found a post from Finn.

"Looking for a Burning Man ticket," it said.

My heart skipped a beat. I'd heard about the annual event in the Gerlach desert of Nevada. For a week, tens of thousands of people gather as a community to share art, music, self-expression and self-reliance. I knew that on one of the last days, an enormous structure of a man, made of wood was burned, hence the name and it was taking place in three weeks.

I had to act fast.

I wrote a message to say, "Hey Finn, you better not come to America and not see me." For all I knew, he could be going with a new girlfriend, but it didn't take him long to reply saying he was going with two guy friends, and if I wanted to join there were a few extra seats in the RV.

His two friends, Levi and Kenny, had already organized an RV, passes, a camp to join and all the supplies necessary to be self-reliable. All I needed was a ticket, some fun clothes, and a healthy openness for adventure.

I was living off my credit cards at the time, but there was no way I was going to let the lack of money stop me.

Without a second thought, I bought a ticket that night for $777. This was all the evidence I needed to reaffirm my wild manifesting powers.

Burning Man was all I could think about. I had minimal insight into exactly what this festival would bring, however, this added to the excitement of reuniting with Finn and the journey ahead.

∾

The only details Finn gave me was the time he was arriving in San Francisco, so I went online and booked the cheapest flight that would land around the same time. The plan was to meet him in San Francisco and from there we would take the Burner Bus to meet his friends on the "playa", the desert where the festival takes place.

It looked like the universe wanted us to meet sooner. I didn't know till the day of departure that Finn had a layover in Los Angeles and then we'd be on the same flight to San Francisco.

I was first to the gate, early and on edge. I glided up to the counter. "Hi there, I have a random request to get a seat next to my friend. I haven't seen him in years and we happen to be on the same flight together."

The attendant looked at me with a gleam in her eyes, "What's his name? Let me see what I can do." Two minutes later she handed me two tickets and said, "Enjoy the flight."

And just like that, I was sitting with two airline tickets, for myself and Finn, our seats right next to each other. I can't say that I didn't think this day would come because I had always imagined it would. I just hadn't known it would take five years.

When I saw him walking toward me, looking the same way he always had, it was still as if nothing had changed between us in all those years. Here we were meeting at a place that represented freedom, opportunity and adventure, an airport. With a ticket to another land of freedom, opportunity and adventure, Burning Man. Everything lay ahead of us.

The Katie who was getting ready to head out to Burning Man was different to the Katie who met Finn six years ago, or the Katie in New York City three years ago, or the Katie who had seen Finn in Australia just a year and a half ago. She was also different to the Katie who had left South East Asia a year ago, and she was certainly different than the Katie in the Caribbean four months ago. There was a lot that I burned off.

I thought that I wanted to be a stylish part of the fashion world.

I envisioned being the single Carrie Bradshaw in New York City.

I believed I was the fun girl who was always down to party.

I wished to be a super healthy Cali girl.

I pined to be a dedicated monk-like community member.

And I was convinced I was going to be a nomadic world traveler.

Yet quite the contrary, what I wanted most was a place to call home, truly my home.

Burning off is an essential part of fire management and happens when dead undergrowth is removed in a managed burn to reduce the risk of future wildfires and encourage regrowth. I had to go through this process of elimination myself, burning off the layers of who I thought I should be in order to get to who I truly was at my core or else I would have had what if's, FOMO (fear of missing out), and potential fantasies for things to be different. Life at this point, for me, was less about knowing who I was and more about knowing who I was *not*.

A quote by Mooji to put this more poetically. "Step into the fire of self-discovery. This fire will not burn you; it will only burn what you are not."

Chapter 19

BURNING MAN

Being with Finn was like taking the first bite of my favorite meal. Before I could even begin to savor all of its goodness, I was already thinking about how I didn't want it to ever end.

The plane ride to San Francisco was a mixed bag. There he was with his alluring hazel eyes, sun-kissed skin and blonde hair. The airplane's engine thrummed, buffing off the edges of our conversation. Every time our eyes met; I felt a spark burn through me. I can't remember what we talked about, but I know it felt easy and comfortable. It also felt like every word had a double meaning.

Staying in the moment was hard, I couldn't stop thinking about what would happen at the end of the ten days. Would we go back to our everyday lives like it meant nothing, or would this be the beginning of a new chapter?

I wasn't sure how to act. I wanted to be with him and didn't want to come across as needy or desperate. I wanted to be a poised effigy of female energy whom Finn would desire on the playa.

After the short plane ride from LA to San Fran, and an eleven-hour bus ride from San Fran to Black Rock City, Nevada, we arrived at the gates of Burning Man.

"We made it", he said, smiling into my eyes.

I smiled back, but I didn't say anything. I was tense, thinking my ticket was fake and this was all too good to be true. Now the scenario of being denied at the gates of Burning Man could be realized. Think positive, Katie.

A man who appeared to be a ranger with a safari outfit, hat and all, came onto the bus with a handheld ticket machine. He was scanning each ticket as they were presented to him, the device letting out a vibrant beep with each accepted one.

As the beeping noise got closer, my adrenaline was pumping to the point of overwhelm. My fate with Finn was going to be decided by that beep. I clutched Finn's hand until he looked over at me quizzically.

"You ok there?" he asked. I laughed nervously as I watched person after person beep through and now it was my turn.

I handed the ticket over to the guy. He scanned my ticket and I held my breath waiting for him to say, "Ahh no, this one's no good." But instead, after what felt like the longest moment, I heard the beep, and he said, "Thank you, Welcome Home." I let out a shaky breath. I could breathe again.

The Burning Man camp shimmered through the desert heat at the edge of the horizon. It looked small from a distance, but something big was in the air. As Finn and I walked over to where the final bus waited, I heard people shouting.

"If this is your first burn, step aside for initiation."

"Oh god, what does that mean?" I asked Finn, who shrugged and said, "I have no idea." It was his first time, too.

A red-haired woman with enormous breasts straining against a purple top came closer to us. "If this is your first burn, step aside for initiation." She looked at me and Finn with a friendly smile and I nodded.

She pointed to a random patch of dust and I found myself surrendering to a group of first-timers. We were given instructions to make angels in the dust. I dropped down with the others, flocked my arms and legs out as instructed and when I got up, the red-haired woman enveloped me in a huge hug.

"You're not a virgin anymore. Welcome Home" she said.

I looked over at Finn who was being hugged by another woman and smiled.

"We're home," I said. He nodded and smiled, dust smudges on both cheeks.

Hugging strangers saying welcome home would have felt forced and inauthentic, but there was something different about these people and this place. For some reason, it really felt like home. It felt like everybody's home. No exclusions. No exceptions. No outsiders.

It's hard to describe what Burning Man is but, for me, if there was a heaven on earth this would be it. Burning Man is a place where, for at least a short time, you can truly let go, dropping all your expectations, judgements and worries. Surrendering into every moment with extreme curiosity, openness and unconditional love. You don't need to know anybody's name, what they do or where they are from. Seven square miles of desert filled with 70,000 people all with the same intentions. Connect, play, have fun, serve and leave no trace behind. One of the main principles of Burning Man is radical inclusion, it's deeply embedded into the event and leaves an imprint. You can be anything and everything that you are and be accepted. No matter what.

Black Rock City isn't a campsite and it's not a permanent city either. Each summer it's created by the organizers – brought to life by its citizens with sheer determination, creativity and drive to build and participate in an incredible experience.

Physically, the layout is like a giant clock. The man (the giant wooden statue that burns toward the end) stands directly in the middle so you can navigate easily. Thank goodness or you would certainly get lost. The rest of the city is laid out on a grid using time as the avenues or the straight lines that radiate out from the man.

Each avenue is named to follow the clock. The streets between the avenues are curved and concentric to the Man, named in alphabetical order, starting with "A" behind Esplanade. The camps are set up at two o'clock and ten o'clock. During its ephemeral existence, Black Rock City has tens of thousands of inhabitants with homes, cafés, bars, restaurants, stores, workshops, medical and emergency stations, you name it, it's there!

Our camp was at 4:30 F so we hopped on a shuttle bus that took us closer to our camp and then walked along the avenue admiring the other camps and caravans, shouting out hellos to the people we passed. Finn held tightly to my hand and I was thrilled to be in this incredible place with him. Our camp was easy to find but we weren't sure which RV was ours until we found a brilliant kaleidoscope-patterned piece of tape over a letter addressed to Finn on the side door.

"We are at Distrikt, 9:00 & G - Kenny & Levi."

I looked at Finn and said, "That's cool tape. I wonder where they got that?"

Finn replied, "Yea that must be Kenny's. He loves bright colors and patterns." We went inside to drop our gear and I thought to myself, I'm going to get along with this Kenny character just fine. I respect a man who's not afraid of bright colors.

"Let's go find them," Finn said. We headed straight out and as we passed other Burners, many would call out to us, inviting us into their camps. So, we stopped off, had a mojito, danced with some strangers and then carried on our way. We didn't have our bikes yet so we travelled on foot, soaking it all in until we made it to the man. Then out of nowhere Levi spotted us, skidded to a stop and jumped off his bike. He gave Finn a big hug and then turned to me.

"Hey, I'm Levi," he said, reaching out to hug me.

"Katie," I said. "I've heard good things."

Levi laughed. His dark hair was nearly white with dust but his wide eyes flashed. "Me too," he said, winking at Finn, and another one of those sparks fizzed through my body.

"Kenny's back at the RV," Levi said to Finn. "He's getting your bikes ready. You can't be walking – you need a bike!"

Levi raced off and as we rounded the corner to our camp twenty minutes later, I saw a shirtless man out front of our RV. He was decorating my pink bike with lights, wearing faded blue jeans shorts with fluorescent green suspenders hanging down on each side and white ski goggles pushed upon his forehead. He looked up as we got closer, a massive grin on his face.

He had blondish brown hair with a moustache and a beard with ginger through it. He was shorter than Finn but broad like a barrel.

"Ah, you made it," he said, giving the bike's kickstand a nudge and coming over to Finn for a big hug.

"Finally," Finn said. "It was a long trip."

"Damn straight, Levi and I waited 18 hours in a traffic jam to get to the playa," he said. He looked at me, "Hey, I'm Kenny."

"Katie," I said. "Thanks for fixing up my bike."

"No worries," Kenny said and leaned in for a hug. This place was full of huggers. I loved it.

In the RV it was me, Finn, Levi and Kenny. Levi also had some friends in an RV across from us in the camp –mainly from England yet residing in Australia like himself. Anna was brunette and chatty, Laura was blond and perky, Leanne was stylish and sweet, and Mick was like the brother we always wanted. We were officially now a family of eight.

At Burning Man there is no money. People who attend give gifts, provide food or perform as part of their participation – everyone is expected to participate. It's just another part of radical inclusion. That night our little family went out and immersed ourselves in the burn culture. We started at a party that was in half an airplane with the DJ up on the flight deck. We saw our first art carts – giant moving pieces of art that would travel around the streets of Black Rock City, shooting flames or full of beach balls. My favorites were a shark cart that blew fire out the side, and another in the shape of a skull. At night they were all lit up and usually belting music.

Even though it was pitch black in the desert, everything was decorated with lights. It seemed like the world was alive with moving and dancing lights. Finn and I stayed near each other the whole time, and as we lost ourselves to the burn, we got closer and closer to each other. I couldn't believe this was happening, I felt I had manifested this dream into life.

After partying hard, I was surprised at how little of a hangover I had the next morning. I was just too happy to focus on anything negative. The boys were slow and sluggish so I made us all banana and peanut butter smoothies. Finn took his with a sleepy, "Ta." Levi passed and Kenny responded with enthusiasm. "Wow, this is tasty. Thanks, Katie. Exactly what I needed!" It was like I had handed him a winning lottery ticket.

On some days Burning Man had themes and Tuesday was all about the tutu. I renamed it Tutu Tupac Tuesday as I wore my black tutu with a bright yellow mid-drift Tupac sweater and a black bandana tied around my head. Me and Finn biked around the playa during the day to check it out and see art installations. You have to see them to appreciate them – but imagine a house on legs, that looks like it could simply take a step and walk away. Or giant purple armadillos filled with foam. It was creativity on crack and pictures couldn't do it justice.

We found ourselves in our first dust storm that morning. It came out of a clear sky in what seemed like moments. It reminded me of being outside in the middle of a snowstorm, silent and blinding. You couldn't see your hand reaching out in front of your face and people would appear out of nothingness. Goggles and masks were necessary to see and breathe, it was like nothing I had ever experienced.

Later that evening, me, Finn and Kenny went out. Levi was off by himself. He was called the traveler, always on the go and the other part of our crew went to bed early. We danced all night and headed out to the deep playa to watch the sunrise while in front of the Robot Heart cart.

I found myself alone with Kenny as Finn danced off in the crowd. It was the darkest part of the night, the time when the playa really came alive.

"This is awesome," I said to him, as we danced around the water bottles below us.

"Yeah," Kenny said. "I wish I didn't live so far away; I would come every year."

We danced for a while when a man came by and handed us each a small stick of Chapstick, saying only "for you", before smiling and walking on. The music turned from fast thumping beats to a slower melody.

I put the Chapstick on.

"Cherry," I said to Kenny laughing. I don't know why I found that hilarious.

"Mmmm," Kenny said, smearing some across his lips.

"So, why isn't Melissa here?" I asked. I'd heard him talk about her briefly and assumed she was his girlfriend but I didn't know any details.

"She lives in New York," he said. "I'm going to meet up with her after, but this isn't her thing."

"Wait," I said, slow on the uptake, "she lives in New York and you live in Sydney? How does that work?" I was curious since this was the exact situation that Finn and I were in.

"Well, it doesn't work well," Kenny said laughing. "It's hard to keep things going and we're constantly trying to figure it out." He paused and watched people dance by in their fur jackets. "It's tough," he finished, looking at me.

"Yeah, well Finn and I aren't together," I said, shrugging. "We haven't been for a long time."

"I'm sure everything will work out for you guys," Kenny said. "Long-distance is not easy. Most of the time I'm not even sure it's worth it. We keep trying to make decisions about me moving to New York or her moving to Australia, but it doesn't seem either one of us is willing to make the big change. And that means we can't move forward. But at the end of the day, I love her."

"Yeah, I get that," I said.

"Finn and I had similar issues," I said. "You probably already know." I looked at him and he shook his head.

"I don't know much. I've only known Finn since he was with Sarah. What happened?"

"Just the usual long-distance crap, I guess. It got harder and harder to find the time to talk and connect. Well, and then he cheated on me." I paused. "Just after I found out my mom had cancer." I looked around the playa, not wanting to meet Kenny's eyes.

"So, I guess there was that," I said.

"What? I didn't know that. I'm sorry to hear about your mom. That's shit," Kenny said quietly. I wanted to hug him right then and there, as I could sense his genuine care even though I had only known him for 48 hours.

"Yea, it didn't feel good at the time, but it's all in the past," I said, shrugging my shoulders. After a few silent seconds, I stopped dancing, looked him in the eyes and said, "Thank you for listening."

Kenny stopped dancing himself and with a sincere face, he said, "Anytime Katie."

Finn danced up then. He wiggled his hips and tossed us each a bottle.

"What is it?" I asked.

"Who knows!" Finn laughed.

I looked over at Kenny who was already unscrewing the lid and taking a swig. "Who cares. Look at where we are!" he added.

I took a big swig. "Right. Who cares!"

That night, I bonded with Kenny. He understood about Finn, and I understood what he was going through with Melissa. We were both emotionally involved with people on the opposite side of the globe.

Things weren't moving forward with Finn though. We acted like a couple but there was never an opportunity to talk. We were always with the others, and the RV wasn't the place for anything private. The longer we were together at Burning Man, the closer we got to the end of the week, and the more anxious I became.

I also found myself wanting to be around Kenny more, he was a great listener and it was a relief to have someone to talk to about Finn. I remember telling Finn how great I thought Kenny was multiple times that week. Though I didn't know, Kenny was saying the same things to Finn about me.

In some ways, Kenny and I became like the parents of our little group, making sure our team of eight was well-fed and had plenty of water at all times. We would fight over who was going to wash the dishes or clean up the RV. We worked well together as a team and had fun doing it. I felt like I could trust Kenny with anything.

I got an inkling that Kenny felt the same way the day he crushed his finger while packing up some scaffold at the camp. I heard him grunt with pain.

"Are you OK," I asked.

"Yeah. I think so," he said. But I could tell he was hurting.

"Let me see." I walked over and reached out for his hand.

Kenny didn't want to show me but I gently tugged his hand until he let me take a look. -

"God that looks awful," I said. "Let me help you."

Kenny is known as Capable Ken because he's the one you go to for help. He's not the one who accepts it. But that day he gave in to me and let me help him clean up his hand and get bandaged up. I was surprised by how good it felt that he trusted me to help him when he needed it.

∼

One night we were all riding home from a long dusty afternoon at Pink Mammoth, exploring the themed camps, when the chain on my bike fell off. I stopped and yelled for Finn but he was far ahead with the rest of the group and didn't hear me.

I started pushing my bike, upset that Finn hadn't even noticed when I saw Kenny around the corner. He was coming back to help me and pulled to a stop.

"You OK," he asked.

"My bike chain fell off again, and I can't get it back on," I said. He jumped off his bike.

"No worries," he said. "I'll try to fix it."

I was suddenly angry, at Finn, not Kenny. "You shouldn't have to be the one to come back for me," I said to Kenny. "Where the hell is Finn?"

With each day passing, I became increasingly insecure about my relationship with Finn. I was perturbed that he kept calling me his girlfriend when clearly, I wasn't. I couldn't figure out what his intentions were but at the same time, I didn't have the emotional language or courage to confront him about it. So, it just sat in my belly as anger, like an ember waiting to be ignited.

Kenny said, "Don't worry, you can ride my bike if you need." I appreciated his offer but in a short moment, Kenny capably popped the chain back on my bike and turned it back over for me.

"All set," he said.

"Thanks, Kenny."

"No worries, Katie."

We cycled back to the RV together. That's just the kind of guy Kenny was, he would have come back to help anybody who was missing. Or was there more to this act of kindness?

Riding into the deep playa - Burning Man

Art cart Burning Man

Art cart Burning Man

-Burning Man

Dancing at Pink Mammoth

Photos by: Anita Tomecki

Chapter 20

FIREWORKS

It was our last day at Burning Man. We'd been up the entire previous night – watching the Man burn, dancing, drinking, making best friends with strangers and exploring everything we could find, finally ending with watching the sunrise over the deep playa. The compounding lack of sleep and wildly intense fun was also coming to an emotional crescendo.

We were at Bubbles and Bass, a camp where they served just that, sparkling wine and melodic beats. A girl with long, bright red braids started hanging out with our crew and I got the impression that she was flirting with Finn.

This wasn't something that would usually bother me but, that morning, it did. Champagne wasn't the only thing bubbling. My deepest insecurities were rising to the surface. A feeling that nobody enjoys – fear rooted in jealousy from past pain. The feeling of not being enough fueled the flames in my belly.

I was also dealing with some confusing and conflicting feelings. The ones where I wanted to be around Kenny more. I felt seen and safe with him. I didn't know what that meant. Did I like him more than just a friend? How could that be – I thought I was still in love with Finn, but to have feelings like this maybe meant I wasn't.

We all headed back to the RV to refuel and take a rest before heading back for our final day on the playa. The girl with red braids had lost her friends so we invited her to join us.

The last night, when the temple burns, is an evocative, emotional event. Many people bring artifacts to burn with the temple, mementos or symbols of parts of their lives they want to be free from. Others might bring things that represent painful or traumatic events. They place these within the temple and watch in complete silence as it all burns away.

There is spirituality, emotional release and a belief that things can burn away leaving only what matters behind. Leaving you scoured, cleansed, and open for your subsequent adventures. It's an incredible way to end the experience.

When we got back to the RV, I excused myself to the bathroom and when I came out, I saw Finn sitting alongside our new friend...just a little too close. I told myself that it was nothing to be concerned about but my wounds from our past were potent. I quickly went into the back where the tiny bedroom was and shut the sliding door. Then I felt the tears sliding down my cheeks and I started to sob.

I didn't want anybody else to see or hear but you can't hide much in small spaces. Finn eventually noticed and I heard the door open and shut as he came into the room.

"Katie, are you OK?" Finn asked. I could hear the concern in his voice and I immediately felt frustrated with myself that I couldn't just let it go.

"Can you just leave me alone," I said. "I really don't want to talk about it. I'm fine. Seriously."

"Come on. I don't understand. What happened?" he said, trying to comfort me.

"I'm serious Finn, not right now." I thought if he just went away, I could pull it together, but he didn't.

"Why are you so upset?" he said. "I don't want this to become a fight."

"It won't if you would just leave me alone," I said, aggravated. I pulled open the door and it snapped back. Finn had a look of surprise on his face and now I couldn't hold it in. "You can't understand why I would be just a *little* upset?"

"What do you mean?" Finn said. "We are all just having a good time."

"Yeah, you're just doing your own thing," I said. "Like you always do."

Kenny and the girl were sitting around staring at us. I didn't risk a glance at Kenny.

"Fuck it," I said, stomping down the front of the steps. Finn followed me out. It looked like it was going to be a full-blown quarrel after all.

"Seriously Katie, why does this have to be an argument? I don't get it. Can't we just *be*?" Finn emphasized the "be" as if it had some real meaning.

"Be what?" I asked, shouting now. "Finn, what can we *be*," I emphasized the word just like him. "Do you want me to just *be* your girlfriend?"

I paused and started again before he could say anything. "Seriously, can you just leave me alone?"

But Finn wouldn't go away, and we kept arguing in circles, getting louder and louder. Going nowhere real fast.

At some point Kenny came out to offer us a wrap, thinking food would help us be less hangry. Finn said, "No thanks, mate." I shook my head, arms crossed tightly over my chest, eyes locked on Finn. This argument was a long time coming, and we were raring to go.

"Honestly, what is the point of all this?" I asked him.

"What do you want me to say?" Finn shouted. "I can't change the way things are. And you're always putting that on me."

"Hey," a man and woman were standing at the RV. They were organizers of the camp we were staying at. "You're going to need to settle down, or take it somewhere else," the man said. "This isn't what the burn is about."

"Or you could help pack up the camp," the woman with him said. I could tell she was less than impressed by us. I took the black garbage bag she was holding out.

"I'm so sorry," I said. Finn just stood there looking grim.

"OK," she said. But she didn't mean it was OK. I felt so embarrassed and guilty for causing a scene so I started MOOPing up. MOOP is an acronym for Matter Out Of Place or anything that is not originally of the land. After all, one of the main principles of Burning Man is "to leave no trace."

"Screw this, I'm going to get some sleep," Finn said, stomping off to the RV. I kept cleaning, tears drying as quickly as I made them in the hot, desert air.

Eventually, Kenny came outside and started to help clean up as well. He didn't say much. But what could he say? It was an awkward situation for everyone. When Levi turned up, I could tell he was surprised and confused to find us cleaning along with the other camp members.

"Hey," Levi said. "Why didn't you meet me?" He stood there, goggles dangling from one hand, a confused look on his face.

"Oh shit. I'm sorry Levi," I said. "Things got a little crazy."

"What do you mean?" Levi asked. Kenny came up, handed him a garbage bag and started quietly telling him what had happened. I just kept my eyes down and kept working.

We weren't the only ones with heightened tension. Maybe the lack of nutrition and personal space had affected us all. Something was going on with our friends in the other RV. And Kenny had some trouble with a couple of the camp organizers so the drama between Finn and I was just part of a bigger picture.

It was time to go.

~

The next morning, we packed it all up and headed to Reno. Most of the people we knew were headed to there for decompression parties, and even though we were over the party at this point, we had committed to going. The pinnacle of all festivals had just happened. You could tell on everybody's faces that we were all tired and could use some quality time to replenish the body and soul; however, there was still Reno to get through. Something was telling me this squeeze wouldn't be worth the juice.

Our family of eight plus the girl with red braids went out to a Mexican place that night. During dinner, she asked me if I was Finn's girlfriend.

"No," I said firmly. "I live in L.A. and he lives in Sydney. We are NOT a couple."

"Oh," she said. "I thought you were." She shot a glance at Finn who was shooting daggers at me.

"Maybe we haven't said that explicitly…" he said.

"No," I said before he could even finish. "We didn't say it explicitly or in any other way."

I was annoyed that he couldn't understand why I would be bothered by the fact that he was calling me his girlfriend. Our definitions didn't match up and I don't play pretend.

I reached my tipping point when we got back to the hotel.

Kenny could sense the tautness in the air so he awkwardly said "I'm going to get some ice for drinks."

"I'll come with ya," I said as I stood up. I wanted to vent about Finn… again.

"Sure," he said.

We went out of the room and down the hall to grab some ice and as we were walking back, I blurted out, "I don't deserve this. I deserve to be with someone like you. Someone who would treat me with more respect."

We stopped in front of the door. I looked up at Kenny and was surprised to see his eyes welling with tears. What could have triggered this emotional response? He reached into his pocket to grab the room key and said, "Yea yea, I know." Before I could ask him what was going on, he'd opened the door and walked in. Finn was lying while watching TV and I realized I was more curious about what Kenny was thinking and feeling than Finn. That burning fire inside me knew that those glossy eyes meant something I had been feeling as well, but I couldn't possibly start that conversation right now.

Chapter 21

KINDLING

The fairy tale with Finn was coming to an end yet again. He was going back to Australia and I was staying in America. We vaguely discussed the idea of meeting halfway in Hawaii for a holiday but with no concrete plans, it felt like this was the end.

Our goodbye at the airport was unemotional, and as I watched Finn walk down the airport concourse, I was left with an unsettled feeling.

∽

Finn and Kenny landed back in Sydney early on a Monday morning and it wasn't long before I got a message from Kenny asking if we could FaceTime to say hello.

"Hey, Katie." Kenny was in the office, wearing a white collared shirt with a red and white polka dot tie. It was strange to see him in professional attire after I had just spent a week in the desert with him wearing bright tights and fur jackets!

'Hey," I said. "You look great."

"Thanks. I'm pretty jet-lagged, but you know… work."

"Yeah. How does it feel to be back?"

"It's nice to be able to get good coffee again."

I laughed. Australians were always complaining about American coffee. "I'm sure. Have you heard from Melissa?"

"Not really," Kenny said. "Just texts to say I made it home OK. What about you and Finn?"

"Nope. Nothing."

We were both quiet for a minute.

"I have to get back to it, but do you think it's cool if we keep in touch?"

I said, "Yea, why not? We did some quality bonding after all." I laughed, and so did Kenny, but after we hung up, I sat a while in silence, feeling perplexed.

A few days later I had a message from Finn saying he had a great time and thanked me for putting him up while in Los Angeles. The informality of the message made me realize that Finn and I had both held onto this romantic idea of "us," but it was more of an idea than a reality. We weren't in the same place and it was clear we wanted different things, but what had changed for me in those previous two weeks?

Life moved on. I went back to nannying, working out and meditating in my closet. I also started talking to Kenny nearly every day. We talked about everything, anything and nothing. Part of me knew that this wasn't just a friendship – but the thought that I could like Kenny more than a friend was crazy. Besides living in Australia, he was friends with Finn, and still trying to make things work with Melissa. I was trying to simplify my life not complicate it, and I couldn't help but fear that this would end up a Finn 2.0. But the more we talked and got to know each other, the more I couldn't deny how I felt about him.

I called Amanda to talk. She knew what was going on – she knew everything, including how I'd felt about Finn over the last few years and the fact that I had texted her the second day at Burning Man saying, "I think I'm in love with Finn's friend. I'm kidding, sort of kind of, but not really."

"Hey," she said, answering on the third ring. I could hear background noises of chatting and laughing and knew she was in the corner bar near her house.

"Hey! What's up?"

"Just out with the boys," she said, "hold on." I could hear some murmuring and then a few seconds later the bar noises changed to the outdoor noises of NYC – cars, honks, and the occasional siren.

"OK, I can hear you now," Amanda said. "What's going on?"

"Not much. Just got off FaceTime with Kenny," I said.

"You guys have been talking a lot?"

"Yeah," I said.

"Girl." That one word said it all.

"I know." I paused. "Do you think I like him just because he's not here? You know, physically unavailable?"

Amanda laughed.

"Maybe that's why I liked Finn all these years, too?"

"God, NO! You like Kenny because he's nice. He's a good guy. You get along. And he likes you, too."

I let out a breath. "You're right."

"Ha, so you DO like him."

I guess it was time to admit it.

Looking back over my life, I couldn't help but find a trend. Whether physical, mental or emotional – in some ways I was attracted to men who were not available and I was afraid that maybe I was continuing a cycle or perhaps I was the unavailable one. I am an all-or-nothing kind of gal and at that moment, I had to admit that I was all in when it came to liking Kenny.

I hadn't felt romantically attracted to Kenny at Burning Man, I just liked being around him, which wasn't surprising. Everyone loved Kenny. But now things were different. It was more serious. It had become my routine to talk to Kenny each day, and after a week, I figured the best way to handle this, was to be honest. I had to get it out of my system or my fire would become uncontrollable.

This was not something one does over a text, but I completely chickened out and sent him a message instead of a phone call.

"Hey Kenny, I don't know how to say this or explain it, but I think I like you more than just friends. I know it might seem crazy considering the situation, but I need to let you know. I'm not expecting any response, but I just needed you to know for my sanity."

I pushed send, feeling my heart pound in my chest. I didn't have to panic for very long because he immediately texted back.

"Could you tell that I felt the same? I didn't know how to bring it up. Let's talk later. xxx"

Later that night we FaceTimed and it was very obvious we both had feelings. All we could do was just see where it took us. I knew, regardless of Kenny, I needed to cut communication with Finn.

I was apprehensive before that call with Finn but I got it out. I told him I didn't think we should talk anymore since we weren't pursing a relationship and were never friends to begin with. It felt like closure (finally) and a conversation I should have had a long, long time ago.

Finn took it in stride and respected how I felt. We had some laughs, he wished me the best and we got off the call. I felt emotionally exhausted for such a short conversation but relieved and clearer.

I didn't tell Finn about Kenny though I doubt he'd have been surprised. I felt Kenny and I needed space to figure out what was between us first. We didn't want to jeopardize the innocence of our relationship, we wanted to keep it pure – based on our feelings, not hindered by anyone else's strong emotions.

At the same time, Kenny and Melissa ended whatever was happening between them. So, me and Kenny decided that we were now officially exclusive. It felt strange to call Kenny my boyfriend when we had never kissed, or even held hands, but it also felt like I had known him my entire life. It was an honest, open, and loving relationship from the start. I was with someone who was committed to communication and forgiving of me, ALL of me.

Kenny and I would FaceTime a few times a day, sometimes for hours. I don't remember talking on the phone that much to anybody in my life. Not even Amanda. I guess we were online dating, which was a first for both of us and we had a newfound respect for it. What we had was special. The more we talked the more it fueled our conversations and we worked on the most fundamental foundations of a relationship: trust, respect, communication and commitment.

All this time talking meant it wasn't long before we were aching to see each other. So, Kenny booked a flight to Los Angeles for a week. He told his roommates he was going away for work and the only ones who knew what was going on were my roommates.

Our online relationship wasn't always tranquil. There were a few times when this was tested. Before Kenny flew out both of us ended up kissing someone else within a few days of each other. It wasn't planned, and it certainly wasn't done out of spite or resentment. It just happened. We'd both had too much to drink and made a poor decision. The conversations weren't fun to have but we both understood our circumstances and that we hadn't even kissed each other yet. We didn't take it personally.

Kenny learned from his one mistake. But it took me a little bit longer, like always.

FaceTime with Kenny
LA --> Syd

Chapter 22

TWIN FLAMES

To understand myself, I turned to the world of personal development and spirituality. I read everything I could about letting things go, living in flow and attracting what you want. I tried to put what I learned into practice, though I didn't always feel successful. One thing that kept piquing my interest was information about twin flames. Something inside told me to pay attention.

Anybody can be your soul mate — a friend, lover or family with whom you share similar energy. A person can have multiple soul mates in life. A twin flame is different; it's the other half of your soul. As the theory goes, at the time of death or after leaving the physical body, a soul can split into two bodies and be reincarnated as two separate beings after its split.

When you encounter the person who carries the other half of your energy, it can create a profound and life-altering sense of wholeness. The most important thing to note is that each person is still whole on their own. A twin flame does not complete you but encourages you to be more complete in your own right.

Your twin flame will elevate your self-knowledge, including knowledge of your flaws, which means there's potential for conflict as well as happiness. Your relationship with your twin flame may or may not be easy and while every relationship teaches you something, your twin flame will teach you the most, especially about yourself.

There are many signs to indicate a twin flame—a strong feeling of recognition, a sense that you've come "home" because you have an immediate and intense connection that is almost psychic, the ability to feel yourself authentically. Twin flames complement each other (yin and yang) and push each other to do better.

These signs were enough for me to recognize my twin flame when he appeared. One thing I wasn't ready for was a few of the tumultuous stages twin flames must go through in their relationship. According to Mind Body Green, a lifestyle brand dedicated to helping people live their best lives, the eight stages of twin flames are yearning, meeting, the honeymoon phase, challenge, test, chase, surrender and coming home.

During the challenge and test stages, things can get tricky. The honeymoon phase is over, and now egos become involved making it common for twin flames to split and, when one pulls away, enter into the chase period. While this is typically a temporary situation, sometimes it can be permanent. Surprisingly not all twin flames are meant to be with one another, at least not physically in this lifetime. If they are meant to be, they enter the final two stages: surrender and coming home.

But first, one essential piece of my twin flames puzzle was to be tested. Were we physically compatible and could our flames burn alongside one another?

Chapter 23

HEAT

On the day of Kenny's arrival, I was a ball of nervous energy. As I pulled up to airport arrivals my head buzzed. What should I say? What do we talk about? How will I feel when I see him again? I even stressed over my welcoming outfit. In the end, I resorted to a plain white T-shirt with blue jeans and a brown leather jacket. Classic, minimal, and just me. As with all airport pickups at LAX, it was curbside, and when I laid eyes on him, he was wearing almost an identical outfit.

It was surreal when we first hugged. My awareness was heightened. I couldn't believe he was really in my arms. We had gotten to know each other so well yet ultimately; we were strangers having only met three months ago. We kissed for the first time outside the airport, awkward but sweet. We climbed into the white whale and went to lunch at one of my favorite Sushi spots, Sugarfish in Marina Del Ray. The tension of two people meeting in earnest for the first time meant our appetites were dulled. The thought of sake at 11 am to lubricate the conversation didn't seem like the suitable launchpad for the next five days.

Luckily, my roommates were gone that week and we could get to know one another comfortably before heading down to the beach with a bottle of red wine and a blanket for sunset. It was almost winter and there was a chill in the air. The beach was deserted of sunset strollers. With the comforts of the blanket, wine and the serene sound of waves breaking on the shore, we stayed at the beach for hours. With every minute we knew our connection was real.

Later that night, we found ourselves compatible in the most romantic way possible. It was a simultaneous climax, organic and loving to the point where it felt like a dream.

It was Thanksgiving so we decided to escape the bedlam of Santa Monica and its influence on the purity of our courtship with a trip to Joshua Tree. We'd spend a night in the desert, like when we first met. Just us, the full moon, a fire, and some fermented grapes. We rented a tiny trailer on a desolate hillside on the outskirts of the national park dotted with sagebrush and cacti. It was equipped with a small kitchen area enough for two people, a covered porch, an outside bathroom and an impressive wood stack to keep our firepit burning all night long. There was no denying our chemistry and ability to have fun together. Our conversation never dried up.

Despite how fluid the relationship felt, we still had the issue of living on separate continents and the unaddressed hurdle of Finn. But for now, we were together and wanted to enjoy it.

On the last night of Kenny's stay, he cooked a tasty meal as we binge-watched Making a Murderer and everything felt effortless. I kept thinking; this is *it*. It has to be. This is how it is supposed to be right? That old saying when you know, you know. We pinched ourselves and both agreed that this was nothing like each other had felt before. There was no question…we both wanted this.

Our goodbyes at the airport were wrenched with emotion. We were both crying and devastated at the thought of parting. Kenny was still in the air en route back to Australia when I booked a flight for him to come back at Christmas. In those three weeks from Thanksgiving to Christmas, we spent more and more time talking about how to be together.

We agreed that it made more sense for me to move to Australia so we sought advice from an immigration lawyer. Our best option would be to get married soon, which felt outlandish until I got a message from Miguel, who said he would be in Las Vegas with his partner Lawrence over Christmas break to see Britney Spears in concert. Las Vegas is only a four-hour car ride from Los Angeles. An idea began to form in my head.

On the phone with Kenny, I suggested we go to Las Vegas when he lands on Christmas Day to meet up with Miguel and Lawrence, who are family to me. Being married by Elvis began as a joke.

"We really should," said Kenny. He was laughing.

I was laughing, too. "How funny would that be!" I said. Then I thought, could he be serious? Could we?

"Wait, are you being serious?" I asked.

"Not really," he said, shrugging. "But we could. I mean, it's legal, right."

"Right," I said. "And it's something that we're going to do anyway."

"Wait, are you being serious now?" Kenny asked.

"I'm not sure," I said laughing again. "I think so."

And then the tone changed, and Kenny became serious. "Wouldn't you want to have a wedding with all your friends and family there?" All joking aside.

"I've never cared about having a wedding. I've never thought about it. It's not something I ever thought I would do. I don't care how we do it. But if it means we can be together…absolutely!"

Kenny smiled. "Well then that's it!"

Wait a minute? Were we really going to do this? I never really believed in marriage but I always said if I were ever to get married, I would elope in Vegas.

As we spoke more, the idea became more real. We couldn't deny how we felt about one another and organically, things began to fall into place. I called Amanda and asked her if she would meet us in Vegas. I knew I would want her there, if we did get married.

She bought a ticket without even a question and asked her cousin Kristy to join. Every day I would go back and forth thinking "yes, this is a good idea" and then "no, it's too crazy." I kept saying things like, "I don't even have a dress." And "if I'm only going to do it once, I want it to be special." But then I'd think, "I never really cared before, why would I care now?" I just didn't know what to do. But at the end of the day, Amanda brought me to my senses (yet again).

"You have to go with your gut, Katie. Do whatever makes you happy but make sure you're listening to your heart, not your head." The fear was in my head but the courage was in my heart. I knew that marrying Kenny would make me happy despite the risk.

Kenny is a traditional man in many ways, so he emailed my dad to ask for permission. He would have loved to do this in person, but unfortunately, this wasn't an option. I am not sure what the email said but it seemed like a kind and cordial exchange, and Dad supported my happiness. I was touched that

Kenny would even think to do this and it made me feel even better about our decision.

And then I almost ruined everything.

A week before Christmas, I went out with a friend, Noah, who was visiting from Europe. Noah and I had travelled together around Australia and New Zealand, and he visited me in New York City. Our friendship was always exactly that… a friendship, completely amicable, nothing physical.

But that night we both got drunk and kissed at an ugly Christmas sweater party. I immediately knew it was wrong, and despite how drunk I was, I broke it off quickly and left the party. I was flooded with guilt and shame.

I woke up the next morning full of anxiety and drowning in regret. I knew there was no grey area here. I was cheating on Kenny this time, and a week before we were meant to be getting married.

Kenny knew what had happened already; I'd sent drunk texts the night before. Of course, I told him everything, I never wanted to lie. I sobbed and cried my way through it, while he sat there hurt on the other end of the line half a world away.

"I'm so sorry, Kenny. You can't know how shit I feel." It took him a few terrible minutes to answer.

Finally, he said quietly, "I forgive you, Katie."

"You do?" I asked, gulping for air through my tears.

"I do. But look, Katie, I also don't want to be a fool. Is this going to keep happening?"

I caught my breath. Was it? This was my moment of clarity. I thought I had my drinking under control 99% of the time, but I was afraid of what that 1% of the time would do. I had grown up with a mom with issues I could see in myself. Did I want to abandon my values and disregard the ones I cared for?

I was my mom's spitting image and I felt like I was so much of her, but this was a side that I didn't want to emulate. I didn't want to risk ending up in someone else's bed and I didn't want to self-sabotage anymore. That was the old Katie, and it was time I said goodbye to her. That night – and Kenny's question – was the last straw.

I took a deep breath and said to Kenny, "No. No, it's not." At that moment I decided I had to get serious about my drinking. Right then and there I made a conscious promise to myself that I would contain and control my experiences by setting better boundaries.

Kenny forgave me but most importantly he put his trust back in me without holding any resentment. I was grateful and wanted to instill that trust back in myself and our relationship. It wasn't like any other relationship I ever had. It felt like we could adequately communicate like adults with real feelings without being volatile.

On Christmas morning, I arrived at the airport wearing a Santa hat with "Kenny" painted in red on the white fur brim. It felt good to see him, hug him and have him close by. We dropped his suitcases off at my apartment and headed straight down to the beach.

As we landed on the boardwalk, we leaned against each other, staring off into the churning ocean. Kenny quickly turned to face me, his back against the water. I thought he was blocking the wind from getting to me because I'm always so cold but he held me close and said, "If we are going to get married, you have to have a ring." He pulled out a vintage gold band with a marquise-shaped sapphire surrounded by diamonds and said, "Will you marry me?" I wasn't shocked but I also wasn't expecting it. Without any hesitation, because there was no doubt in my mind, I said, "Yea, of course." And just like that, we were engaged.

Later that night we drove out to Las Vegas to meet Miguel and Lawrence. Amanda and Kristy were flying the next day. We left later than planned and in perfect LA fashion, we hit massive traffic. Since we had time in the car, I called my godmother, Aunt Rose, the closest thing I had to a mother figure.

"Hey Aunt Rose," I said.

"Hey, Kate!"

"So, I'm just calling to let you know that Kenny and I are heading out to Vegas right now."

"Oooh, I love Vegas," she said. "Pull a slot for me, OK honey?"

"Of course! But I also wanted to tell you that we're thinking about getting married while we're there."

"Really?" Aunt Rose asked.

"Yep. We're not a hundred percent sure yet, though."

"Well, good for you," she said. "As long as you're happy Kate, that's all that matters. And don't worry about where you get married. I got married to your uncle in my Pizza Hut uniform, on my lunch break." And then she started laughing. I could always count on my family to take the seriousness out of situations.

When you go through enough trauma, you realize the fragility of life and the importance of enjoying as much as possible, while you still have the chance. I knew that my entire family would support any decision I made. Kenny's parents were supportive as well. It was comforting to know we both had family support.

We didn't arrive in Vegas until after nine pm. I'd booked us a standard room at The Palms Hotel, and because we got there so late on Christmas Day and all the rooms were booked, they had to honor our reservation with the penthouse suite. We couldn't believe it. We had an entire suite to ourselves with a fireplace, three bathrooms, a kitchen, a living room and a dining room on the top level of the Palms.

We only had it for one night so let's just say we made the most of the room and stayed in. Those blackout curtains were a plus!

When we checked out, we decided to stay at the same hotel Miguel and Lawrence were staying at, The Linq. It was right on the strip and the only hotel that allowed dogs since Lawrence had brought his Yorkshire Terrier, Manny. We were still thinking about the wedding but I didn't have a dress and we hadn't ironed out any details.

We joined the boys as they headed down to Planet Hollywood for the Britney concert and after they left us, we continued into the Magic Mile Mall. The first shop we saw had a rack of sale clothes outside, so I started to skim and immediately found a white lace tube top dress. I tried it on and it fit like a glove.

I looked at Kenny and smiled. "Well, I have a dress now, I guess we can get married tomorrow." Kenny had brought a suit for himself just in case. But wedding or no wedding, it was Saturday so when the boys got back from the Britney concert, we had a big night out.

The next day, no one made their way out of bed until the afternoon. Kenny and I went down to reception to book another night but there was no availability, so I rebooked us at The Palms hotel.

Before I left the counter, I asked the receptionist, "Out of curiosity, do you have any recommendations on where to get married, preferably not an Elvis thing."

She smiled at me and Kenny. "The Flamingo next door has a lovely garden chapel," she said. "Couples who get married there seem very happy."

I looked at Kenny. "What do you think?" I asked.

He smiled and took my hand. "Let's go check it out."

We walked over and they had one appointment left for the day, the last slot at 4:30 pm. We took it. We had exactly two hours to go downtown, pick up the marriage license, check into our hotel off the strip, shower, get ready and then take a taxi back to the strip. We didn't really have time to think. I just remember rushing around hoping we wouldn't be late.

When we were in our hotel room getting ready, I was finished before Kenny so I called Dad.

"Hey Dad," I said. "I just wanted to let you know that it's happening. Kenny and I are getting married at 4.30 pm."

"As long as you're happy, Kate, that's all that matters. And don't worry about what anybody else thinks. I love you."

I got off the phone feeling confident and sure. Then moments before we walked out of our hotel room the song "Canon in D Major" started playing on Kenny's playlist, the music that plays just before the doors open for the bride to walk down the aisle. I felt chills. Not that I needed another sign of confirmation, but there couldn't have been better synchronicity.

We arrived ten minutes late, but it was ok as the chapel staff were still getting the hall ready. I had a dressing room intended for the bride and her bridal party, so it was big enough to fit at least ten people comfortably. Kenny and the boys had to wait outside on the couch.

Amanda, Kristy and I were all ready to go and as we waited, we laughed about our antics the night before. Kenny slotted so easily into my world of friends. Miguel, Lawrence and Manny, came in for a hug and to wish me luck. Amanda pulled them in saying, "We need photos!"

We posed around the room, laughing and joking. It was fun and felt normal. Miguel made his usual inappropriate jokes, taking any pressure or worry away, which is one of the many qualities I love about him.

"How's Kenny," I asked Miguel after we'd finally put the camera away.

"Oh, Kenny left," he said with a stone-cold look, "that's what we came in here to tell you." I knew never to take anything Miguel told me seriously.

I began to get nervous when someone from the chapel popped in to give me a bouquet of fake white roses to hold. It was getting real. Then the man who would be marrying us came in. He was a tall, slender man in his early sixties with a good amount of grey hair left on his head. He introduced himself as David, my father's name, so I took that as another divine sign.

"So, you're getting married today?" He had a nice way about him – comfortable and kind.

"Do you want a religious or civil ceremony?"

"Oh, civil for sure," I said. "I'm spiritual but I'm not religious."

"That's fine," he said, smiling his reassuring smile. "It's going to be a beautiful wedding. I'll see you out there." A woman came in a few minutes later and said they were ready.

I grabbed Amanda's arm and smiled at her. She was going to walk me down the aisle instead of my faja. She had been the closest person to me for the past six years and I couldn't imagine where my life would have been without our friendship. She was with me through everything and I was thankful to have her there that day.

Kristy, Miguel, Lawrence and Manny went into the hall where Kenny and David were waiting. Amanda and I stood outside the doors to the chapel waiting for the cue. I felt butterflies, but they were butterflies of excitement. Any nerves I had were long gone.

As soon as the doors opened, someone on the piano started playing "Canon in D Major." I hadn't seen the chapel before, so I was surprised that the room decor wasn't the Vegas tacky I'd been imagining. It had a simple yet artistic white circular symbol on the front wall with a group of white candles glowing gently below it.

I had no idea we would have a professional photographer there, but he started snapping photos as soon as we walked in. Thankfully it was a short walk from the door to Kenny. Even though there were only eight other people and a dog in that room, it was nerve-racking with everyone looking at me. I don't know how people do large weddings.

Kenny started tearing up by the time I was mid-way down the aisle. Once we got to Kenny, I hugged Amanda, then turned to him with a big smile and squeezed his hands. I was standing to the left. Amanda, Kristy, Miguel, Lawrence and Manny were all sitting to the right so I could see them out of the corner of my eye.

Me and Kenny both turned to face David. The music stopped and David started with a quote from Rumi, "Lovers don't finally meet somewhere. They're in each other all along."

My nerves calmed. This was the perfect quote for us. I felt Kenny and I had known each other for so much longer than four months. We had been with each other all along.

Kenny was tearing up so much that when David said the vows and asked Kenny if he could say I do, Kenny struggled to get the words out so I said, "I do" thinking it didn't matter who said it first. David chuckled and said, Kenny, has to say it. Then Kenny laughed and said "I do" wiping his eyes. And then it was my turn, and I finally got to say "I do" for the second time.

I had forgotten the part of a wedding ceremony where you exchange rings, but Kenny hadn't. He had his grandmother's thick gold wedding band, which completed the ring set. When it came time for his band, I happened to be wearing a thumb ring that magically fit his ring finger. It was a thin silver band with a wing on it, which I'd bought since Kenny's last name is Hawkins and it looked like a hawk wing.

I've learned that planning is essential but plans are ultimately useless and when things feel too hard it's because a greater force is telling me something. In between the planning and the letting go, everything fell beautifully into place.

Getting ready to walk down the aisle

*Wedding Party
Las Vegas*

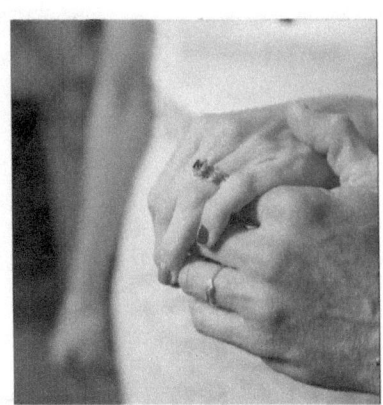

*Wedding Rings
Las Vegas*

Photos by: Imagine Studios: Las Vegas, NV

On seaplane in Syd for 30th Bday

Chapter 24

SMOKEJUMPER

We were married but humble in our new union and didn't post through any social media channels. We still had a lot ahead of us, living in the same country and having the opportunity to socialize with friends as a couple. Finn still didn't know, although Kenny had tried to convey the news on occasion, but struggled to find the right moment.

We felt that Finn had to know at least that we were a couple by this point and maybe things would have turned out differently if I had an honest conversation from the start, but I had hesitations. At first, I'd hesitated for fear of inviting negative energy into mine and Kenny's budding relationship. Then, I felt I didn't owe anybody an explanation of who I loved or why I loved them.

It was eventually addressed when both Finn and Kenny attended a mutual friend's wedding in Australia and had an alcohol-fueled bonding session over a cigarette. Kenny thought it was a good opportunity to ease into the uncomfortable admission of our marriage. So, while passing what they called "the peace pipe" it all came out.

"So, mate, I guess you know about me and Katie," Kenny said.

Finn took a drag on his cigarette and avoided Kenny's eyes.

"Yeah, you guys are together, hey?" Finn said.

"Yeah. We got married just after Christmas."

Finn laughed. "Really? That's awesome. I'm not surprised, I always knew you guys were sort of into each other."

"Well, it wasn't like that," Kenny started. But Finn interrupted.

"It's all good," Finn said. "She's a great girl and I'm sure you guys will be really happy."

"Yeah. She is. I am sorry we didn't tell you earlier," Kenny said.

"Seriously, it's really fine, mate," Finn said, clapping him on the back. "Congratulations."

It seemed like everything was going to be just fine. Finn even sent me a lovely message wishing us the best for the future. I'd be lying if I said it didn't cross my mind that people might think that I married Kenny for a visa or to get back at Finn. Or that Kenny broke the ultimate 'bro-code'. But in the end, whatever people thought didn't matter. I knew my truth, Kenny knew his truth, and together we knew our truth. We were the only ones who mattered. When you are honest and authentic, the judgement of others can't touch you. As Ann Landers once said, "The naked truth is always better than the best-dressed lie."

~

That Valentine's Day, I decided since I couldn't be with Kenny, I was going to run the LA marathon. Love makes you do some funny things! I had never run more than a mile previous to the training, but I trained with a pace group and managed to finish the full marathon in under five hours. Then I had to walk two miles home. In pain. Maybe crying. And that was the last time I ever ran more than a mile in my life.

A few weeks later, for my birthday I flew to Australia and while there Kenny surprised me with an airplane ride over Sydney harbor and the northern beaches. We climbed in the back behind the pilot and slipped on our flight harnesses. The pilot fitted us with headgear that cut out some of the noise, and let us hear the air traffic controllers. We held hands as the plane took off out over the ocean and flew past the harbor.

The day was stunning – a beautiful clear summer's day with a deep blue sky like you see nowhere else but Australia – and I was flying over the city with the person that I loved.

After we bounced to a landing at Palm Beach, we sipped champagne and ate oysters. Watching Kenny grimace as he ate them, I learned that while he loves to order oysters, he doesn't enjoy the texture. It was yet another thing that I loved about him.

My trip to Sydney was only five days long –just enough to get over the jet lag. It was a whirlwind trip trying to get to know Kenny's friends. I knew some of them from mutual friends but it was special meeting his mates that he had known since early school days. All of his friends were down to earth, kind people, solidifying my conviction that Kenny was the type of person I wanted grow old with.

Since I was there, I also thought it was a good time to clear the air with Finn.

On the day, we met at Kenny's apartment across the street from Bronte Beach. Finn stepped out of the Uber, swamped by a big plant. We watched him maneuver up the stairs to Kenny's apartment and when I opened the door, he handed it to me.

"It's a Peace Lily," he said, grinning.

"Thanks," I said. "That's sweet." I put the plant on the table and felt like we were on the right track.

"Good to see you, mate," Kenny said. He and Finn gave each other one of those masculine back thumping hugs and seemed genuinely happy to see each other.

"Do you want something to drink…a beer?"

"Yeah, sure," Finn said.

Kenny went to get drinks and the three of us sat around for a few minutes just chatting. It wasn't awkward or strange at all.

I finally saw Finn for Finn – just another human being – not as this idea or some character I had built up. While he wasn't meaningless to me, our relationship didn't have any "meaning" anymore. I felt completely comfortable with my feelings and the choices I had made.

Finn took a final swig of his beer and set his glass down. I set my beer down as well and turned toward Kenny.

"Do you mind if me and Finn go for a little walk to the beach?" I asked.

"No, not at all, of course." Kenny said.

"Shall we?" I said as I gazed over to Finn.

"Yeah, let's do it," he said.

There was plenty of people out and about as we headed downstairs and across the road to a bench. The conversation had been light and trivial to this point without yet addressing the elephant in the so room so I decided to ask a question.

"So, did you ever sense anything between Kenny and I before he told you?"

"Yeah, me and Melissa both had a gut feeling. We talked about it a little bit after Burning Man," Finn said. "I caught on at Burning Man for sure. You were always saying how awesome Kenny was and Kenny was always telling me how great he thought you were." I wanted to laugh but didn't think that would go over too well.

"Melissa thought so, too?" I asked. "But she wasn't there?"

"She started to get a feeling in San Francisco. Kenny kept talking about how great you were, and how well the two of you got along. He probably thought he was talking about you just like a friend, but Melissa's not stupid."

I wasn't sure what to say.

I felt like Rachel from the show, *Friends* in the episode where she's at the kitchen table clipping flower stems with pregnant Phoebe and she realizes she's in love with Ross again and everybody else knew before her. She stands up and shouts to Phoebe, "Why didn't you tell me I was in love with Ross!?" And Phoebe replies, "We thought you knew; we talk about it all the time."

"You know nothing happened at Burning Man, but we did bond," I said. "And I guess we wanted to keep that bond. So, we just started chatting. We didn't expect anything more to happen from it, especially because he's here and I'm not. But then it just felt really right." I shrugged my shoulders.

I wasn't sure that this was what Finn would want to hear – but it felt good for me to be able to say it to him.

"Yeah, I get that," he said. He was quiet for a minute. "And yeah, I'm happy for you both," he said, smiling.

"Thank you," I said. There was nothing more to say, no animosity existed between us anymore. We were in a good place. It would take another friend's wedding a couple of years later to really bury the hatchet.

∼

Five days passed in what felt like moments, and once again I was filled with sadness to say goodbye. I already felt like my life was in Australia, but at least when we left each other this time, Kenny and I had a clear permanent plan for the future. I would head out to Australia in a few months and we would be together. As the pieces fell into place without effort, I knew I was moving in the right direction.

I moved out of my apartment in Santa Monica and drove back east in the white whale with Amanda. The cross-country road trip was a great way to spend quality time with her before moving to Australia indefinitely. We landed in New Jersey for Kenny's arrival, and now me and Kenny were on a road trip to visit as many people as we could squeeze in.

In New Jersey he met Amanda's family, my Aunt Millie and cousins, then we went down to West Virginia to meet my dad, my brother Rick, his kids, more aunts, uncles and cousins. Then we went to Virginia to meet my brother, Rob, his kids and finally down to Florida to meet my sisters Cassy and Dee, her kids and more extended family.

We had a few days in New York City to meet some friends before we flew out to Australia. The cross-country travel and socializing were no small feat, but Kenny seemed energized by it.

It all went quickly and was sentimental. Everybody loved Kenny and Kenny loved them back. Kenny comes from a small family with just one sister, so I think he found my large family with all its unique American dynamics an interesting novelty. I knew everything was right when I came out of my dad's house to find him standing with Kenny in the garage, chatting about cars. It was like he had been a part of my family for years. My dad has never been hugely social and seeing him and Kenny getting along so well felt amazing.

More than anything, I wished he could have met Mom. I know he would have loved her and she would have adored him. She would have loved to hear him speak in his accent, she'd have asked him to tell her everything about his life and he would have been obliging.

Seeing my family through Kenny's eyes changed the way I looked at them. Maybe I realized that this time I was *really* leaving, for good, or maybe it was just that Australia was *really* far away.

Or perhaps, this was the first time I allowed myself to be vulnerable. I didn't have to be strong anymore, and a big part of me wanted to stay and have more time with them. I felt blessed to not only have a family, but a big family, who didn't care who I married and how I married them, just as long as I was happy. I felt a sense of pride rather than shame, which was a shift from my usual perspective. Whatever the reason, for the first time in my life, I felt real sadness saying goodbye to my family.

At Sukha Mukha Yoga Studio - Bronte

Photo by: Lynn Quiroz

Chapter 25

BURNING IN

"I'll see you later tonight, love you," Kenny said as he kissed me goodbye.

Half asleep at 7am, I lifted my head and said, "Okay, darling, love you too."

I'm on Australian soil, shivering underneath covers at Kenny's childhood home. It's the start of winter and Sydney-siders are allergic to turning on any heat so I would have to rely on the sun for warmth.

Kenny was off to work and wouldn't be home until 7 pm. Even though we had only been at his parent's house for a week, temporarily, until we found a place, my anxiety was getting the better of me. I couldn't get out of my head or stop focusing on everything that wasn't working.

I had just arrived in a foreign country, married to a man I had known less than a year, living in his family home with his two retired parents, an hour and a half away from anybody I knew in Sydney. I couldn't work for months as I waited for my visa, I couldn't drive due to the opposite side of the road thing (plus not having a car), and I couldn't go anywhere or eat anything without running it by his parents. I was way out of my comfort zone and struggling with the lack of independence.

That morning's meditation practice triggered another panic attack. I sat on the bed, crossed-legged with a big wool blanket wrapped around my shoulders. My headphones were in. My mind was racing, jumping from one negative thought to the next when the door opened and Kenny's mom walked in.

Seeing me sitting erect like a statue of Buddha, she said "Oh, I'm so sorry," and turned around, closing the door behind her.

This shouldn't have been a big deal but, at that moment, it felt like I had just been stripped of my last bit of freedom.

Whatever you resist not only persists but goes to the basement and starts lifting weights. My sense of being overwhelmed and my resentment at this predicament had been lifting some heavy weights down in my self-contained subconscious apartment. My emotions came to the surface, but not gracefully or constructively…they erupted like a storm surge. I could feel my heart beating fast, my stomach in knots, and my body shaking even though I was under a warm blanket. The floodgates opened.

I found myself on the bathroom floor again, wishing my reality to be different. I was questioning my entire life, thinking I was in a hole that I couldn't zoom out of and at the same time I was scared to validate or share these feelings with Kenny because I was afraid of being ungrateful. The critic in my head kept saying, "don't be dramatic, suck it up and move on," but the compassionate part said, "it's alright, it's going to be okay, just talk with Kenny."

Instead of going to Bondi that day to see some friends, I saved my energy for an uncomfortable conversation with Kenny when he got home from work.

"We need to talk, Kenny," I said. He could tell by the look on my face, I was upset.

Kenny didn't say anything so I continued. "I can't do anything for myself here and I hate feeling trapped."

Kenny's response was the one that I had feared.

"Katie, you're being ungrateful. My parents are putting us up to help us. It's no one's fault that you can't drive or work. That's just the way it is."

"I'm not saying it's anyone's fault. I'm not blaming anyone," I said. "All I'm saying is that this situation is not ideal for me right now and I'm not in a good head space."

"What exactly do you want me to do?" He sounded offended so I got defensive and said, "I don't know, maybe I shouldn't have moved here so quickly."

He paused and said words that hit my heart like a hammer blow. "Maybe we've both made the worst decision of our lives."

"I never said this was the worst decision of my life, I just feel stuck and need to do something different."

I didn't feel like an imposter who had made a wrong decision. I knew the fears were in my head but my heart was the one keeping score. The reality was simple, we just needed our own space, and fast.

The next day I refocused all that anxious energy on aggressively apartment searching in the Bondi area. The only requirements were natural light, walking distance to the beach and a bus because I was petrified of driving. We also needed something available immediately. It doesn't sound like a long list but it was a hot market, leaving us with quite literally one option.

After inspection, we signed the lease for a sunny 60sqm one-bedroom apartment on Bondi Road, not far from the beach. You couldn't miss the building, painted bright yellow with a small wooden boat outside the front surrounded by palm trees. People called it the Banana Boat building. My favorite part was that it had a community compost and garden.

It didn't have a balcony and we lived next door to what we could only presume were drug dealers. They had parties with loud music and banging going on at all hours of the night. Thankfully, the building was so old it was double-bricked between apartments and almost soundproof. Almost.

Living with Kenny was easy. Easier than I had ever imagined it could be. I had never lived with anybody besides roommates, never mind a "husband." Unfortunately, from what I observed from married couples, they never seemed happy and healthy. It was like they easily got bored and frustrated with one another. But with Kenny, I never felt that way, even though we lived pretty much on top of each other.

Now, in an apartment, with the man I loved, with nature and good friends around me, I started to feel more grounded and interested in healing my body through alternative methods. A friend suggested I go for reiki. Reiki is a Japanese form of energy healing. Reiki practitioners use a hands-on-healing technique through which a "universal energy" is transferred through the palms of the practitioner to the patient encouraging emotional or physical healing.

In my first session, stuff about my mom came up and she suggested I take out my belly ring, explaining that having an unnecessary medal object in my chakra system could create imbalance with the energetic flow. I am all for trying new things so I listened and ever since that day, my gut issues of not just a few years but 30 years are no longer. Maybe it was a coincidence (if you believe in that sort of thing).

In the second session, the reiki practitioner asked me about my sexual abuse. I was taken aback and said, "I wasn't sexually abused," and wondered why she would ask me such an odd question. I never considered what happened to me as abuse and I didn't think about it again until months later when the #metoo campaign came out. It was only then that I admitted…#metoo.

The #metoo movement unexpectedly caused me to re-evaluate events from my past, see them differently and endure a painful reckoning that ultimately helped me heal. For the first time, I started speaking to people I wasn't necessarily emotionally close to but had shared similar experiences. This bred courage to finally talk to close friends and family. Even though they weren't easy memories to process and talk about, shame can only live in the dark and the sunlight is the best disinfectant.

After that second Reiki session, I also had to go to the hospital for a kidney stone. Passing that stone was an excruciating pain I wouldn't wish on anyone but I knew it was my body's way of releasing and shedding. The Reiki practitioner explained that our kidneys filter impurities out of the system, so kidney stones are related to heavy, toxic energies like anger, blame, resentment, fear and shame that haven't been processed. That resonated. Besides yoga and meditation, Reiki was yet another holistic healing technique that showed me it was possible to heal myself, break patterns and move through deep subconscious conditioning.

∼

Transitioning into newlyweds seemed to be working. At times, I was waiting for the other shoe to drop because I just assumed relationships were supposed to be hard, and mostly miserable. But Kenny and I complemented not only our similar shared values but our differences, too. We loved staying in just with each other and at the same time gave each other enough space to breathe and be their own person. And anything that ever happened in the past never came back up.

It wasn't rainbows and puppies all the time. We had our disagreements but I guess I was surprised by how mature and meaningful our relationship truly was, considering how fast everything happened. This is what I had always imagined – an undeniable intense bond that felt like home.

∽

My relationship felt balanced but my work-life felt deranged. I was now 30 years old and couldn't get away from that never ending societal pressure to have an impeccable answer to, "So, what do you do?"

As a true Pisces, I wanted to be involved with some kind of humanitarian work where I could be of service and feel good about what I was doing with my precious time on this planet. Talk about a broad millennial goal.

When I am unsure of what to do next, I reflect and ask myself questions like: what option scares me the most (the scarier the better) and does what I'm about to do take me in the direction I eventually want to be in? Then I ask the universe for signs. "*Signs*" to me are simple synchronicities or events that line up with ease. You will have noticed plenty of them in this book.

Then I remembered Yoga Teacher Training. I had signed up in Los Angeles, but had to cancel because I moved to Sydney. I didn't necessarily want to be a Yoga teacher but I thought this holistic route could plant new seeds. I emailed every Yoga studio I could find that offered Yoga teacher training programs and asked if they had any potential scholarships available because at the time, I didn't have a spare four thousand dollars laying around. After over a month of no responses, I was starting to feel discouraged.

"I don't think it's ever going to happen," I said to Kenny one night while we snuggled on the couch.

"Yeah, it will. Give it time. Trust," Kenny said. I don't know if Kenny was psychic or just lucky, but he was right. The next day a small studio in Bronte, within walking distance, emailed me.

The studio owner, Theresa, informed me she didn't offer scholarship programs, but did have a work-trade option that might suit. She invited me to meet for coffee.

The meeting with Theresa went great and left me feeling eager. I loved her energy, her philosophy of giving back and the fact that she started Yoga when she was living in New York City. I now had a goal and a place to put my attention. I didn't have to know how things would turn out, I just had to keep putting one foot in front of the other.

An inward fire had sparked to life. The way I see it, life is all about managing fires. Some of them I will start, others will be started for me, but it is up to me to make sure I do not get consumed by the fires; otherwise, I'll burn out. I've learned to efficiently maintain and transform my fires so that they are motivating and inspiring, not overwhelming. Keeping me lit from the inside out. Giving me energy to keep *burning in* instead of burning out.

Chapter 26

OXYGEN

Bondi's sunset sky was lit with vibrant streaks of pinks, blues and oranges. It was a week before my Yoga teacher training graduation and I was walking home on a high. My phone had been on silent so that I could fully be in the yoga space all day and when I flicked it over, a message from Kenny caught me off guard.

"*Hey babe, I was offered a job in Brisbane, Queensland, so would you want to move there? Let's chat about it when you get home. Love you xx.*"

My initial thought was, "I love Sydney and we have only been here for a year." Brisbane was so far away; I didn't want to leave all my friends and the community I'd built in Sydney but it didn't take long for my tune to change.

These things are best discussed on calls rather than by text so I called him back.

Kenny answered on the second ring. "Hey, babe!"

I could hear the excitement in his voice and my gut was telling me, change is good and everything happens for a reason. After all, there are two things I have a PhD in moving and adapting. Maybe this was the next step that the universe had planned for us.

"Babe this is crazy!!" I said. "And amazing," I added quickly.

"Can you believe it? It's a great opportunity." He paused. "I've never lived anywhere but Sydney... I think it's time for a change." I could hear the smile in his voice.

His excitement was infectious, and I knew it was the next right step for us.

"Do you remember just a few weeks after we met you asked me if I would ever move to Queensland? Well, my response is the same as it was then... of course, I'll move anywhere with you! It'll be a new and exciting adventure together."

Kenny sighed. "Ah, that's great babe. I'm so glad you support this. I wasn't sure how you would feel, you know since you made such a big sacrifice moving to Australia. But now we can both start fresh somewhere new together. It feels right, feels good."

I laughed. Now, rather than resistance, I felt excitement. What would the next chapter hold for us?

In a few short weeks, we had moved to luxurious waterfront property on the Gold Coast in Paradise Point, an hour and a half south of Brisbane.

Kenny suggested I start teaching Yoga classes for his office buildings and before I knew it, I was teaching ten classes a week.

My confidence still lacked and was evident in my shaky voice, or what sounded shaky to me, but I persevered. Teaching full-time was enjoyable yet it had a shelf-life. Knowing it was unsustainable, I started my own business.

In addition to teaching yoga, I started teaching meditation, facilitating workshops, retreats, and doing Reiki healings. To complement this, I also created a line of eye pillows filled with reiki, crystals and lavender called "Paradise Pillows."

The months went on and even in my line of work, the day-to-day stressors were adding up. The three to four-hour commute each day was physically and mentally draining. It felt like Kenny and I didn't have the time to appreciate each other like we used to. Usually, our differences complemented each other like a coherent yin and yang, but now they were starting to clash. I remember car rides home after a long day where we'd be arguing over what to do about dinner, or on the weekend. It was nothing, but at the same time, it was everything.

The island on which we lived had a weird vibe too. It was paradise in many ways, but it was cut off and felt soulless. The place was filled with retirees and there weren't many new faces around. People didn't walk the streets or make lasting friendships. You might see people getting together to have BBQs, but it felt more like they were on a holiday rather than living real lives. I felt isolated living there.

A few days before we moved in, the neighbors across the hall, a retired mother and her elderly daughters, took their own lives in a suicide pact. The husband of the mother had died in the stairwell at the gym on the island, too. This tragic story just added to the strange feeling of the island. We needed to move.

∽

Strong memories are always tied to strong emotions. It was a Thursday morning, February 8th, when Kenny and I drove to Brisbane together. As the houses and industrial areas along the highway sped past, we sat in uncomfortable silence. We'd gotten into an argument the night before and neither one of us were ready to reach across the divide and make up.

When we arrived in the building at 8:00 am, we didn't even kiss each other goodbye like we normally did. Just a quick, "See you later." Kenny took the elevator to level eight and I stayed on the ground floor in the converted board room which was now the yoga room. It didn't have any windows, but it had high ceilings and once I'd set up my lighting, an oil diffuser and other yogi decorations, it became a peaceful space that I enjoyed.

With spare time on my hands, I was able to work on my website and do some personal admin, but that morning I couldn't concentrate.

I turned to meditation to help me clear out the cobwebs and refocus my energies. I sat with my back against the wall, feeling the need for some support, closed my eyes and focused on my breathing. I felt the air coming in and out of my nose and filling my lungs and chest. I tried to focus only on that, only on my breath, the here and now, but as soon as I did the tears started to flow.

The room was serene but I felt turmoil. Inside I was shouting, "Why can't you be happy and grateful? You're so annoying, get over it already!"

Then a wiser voice said, "Katie, just be vulnerable and talk to Kenny."

The door opened, and Kenny walked in. He could sense my energy and his demeanor changed.

"Hey babe, you okay, what's up?" he said concerned.

I wiped my face and the words I was feeling poured out.

"I just don't feel like we have been a support system for each other. I can feel how stressed you are and I get it but," I sniffled.

"I want to be in a relationship where we fan each other's flames, not dim each other's sparkle."

I knew that last bit about flames and sparkles sounded corny, but Kenny was used to my maniac metaphors. I wiped my eyes again. Just saying the words had made the tears well up again.

He came over and slid down the wall until he was sitting next to me. He took a deep breath and took my hand. Then he looked me in the eyes and kissed me.

"Of course, I don't want to dim your sparkle. I love your sparkle and our sparkle. I love you."

His voice wobbled. I looked at him and could see the tears pooling in his eyes, and I knew he meant what he said. We kissed again, and I leaned against his shoulder.

For that moment everything felt alright. After a few minutes, he got up and went on to his next meeting and I got ready to teach.

∼

I'd finished my classes for the day wearing red tights with a gray oversized sweater and had ducked out for a coffee. I remember the smell of the decaf soy mocha as I slurped it in through my teeth, trying to bring in some air to cool it down. I was walking down a side alley and had just rounded the corner when I saw an ambulance parked in front of the building. An eerie feeling washed over me. Something was wrong.

"Whoever that ambulance is for, I hope they are okay, sending them love and light." I sent my metta meditation out into the universe as I made my way inside. I was only a few steps into the converted yoga room, and I'd just chucked my Birkenstocks off when the cleaner who worked in the building rushed in, wearing black pants, the blue company polo shirt, and a frazzled expression.

"Katie the ambulance! The ambulance is for Kenny! C'mon, I'll take you upstairs."

My breath caught in my throat and my stomach dropped. I jumped up and followed her out of the room, straight into the elevator, barefoot. I was in fight or flight mode. The elevator ride was interminable, and the panic in my heart was exacerbated by the weird corporate calm of the environment.

When the doors opened on level eight, I remember the intense silence. The cleaner didn't say anything, just let me down the hall to where Kenny was, but the look on her face said it was serious. I knew he didn't just break an arm.

When I got to the meeting room, Kenny was lying on the floor. One of the paramedics was holding him under the arms and head. Kenny was still in his blue pants and white shirt however his red tie was off and his shirt was unbuttoned. He couldn't hold himself up and was swaying back and forth in the paramedic's arms. The other paramedic was next to the stretcher.

I remember thinking, "How the hell are these paramedics so calm? Why is no one doing anything?"

I walked over beside him and knelt, putting a hand lightly on his chest.

"I'm here, babe," I said. His eyes were open and bloodshot. It looked like he had been crying for hours. He didn't answer me.

"What the hell happened?" I looked up at the paramedic for the first time.

"Are you his wife?" The paramedic asked. He sounded kind but unruffled. I found his calm demeanor off-putting in comparison to how I felt.

"Yes, I'm his wife. What happened?" Kenny was trying to speak, but I couldn't understand what he was saying. I could tell he understood what was going on but it was like he couldn't get the words out correctly.

"I just saw him two hours ago," I said. "He was fine. Did he have a heart attack? His dad has had a few, and he has been stressed." I knew I was sounding more and more panicked and I took a deep breath, trying to force myself to be calm.

"Ma'am, do you know if your husband has taken anything recently or done anything differently today?"

I racked my brain. What did he eat? Maybe this is just a crazy allergic reaction. Did he take any medications? I couldn't think of anything.

"No, we drove to Brisbane together this morning." I paused, trying hard to focus my mind. "Ummm, he had some Vegemite toast and coffee before we left."

In the paramedic's arms, Kenny just kept swaying. He was tugging at his shirt, trying to pull it off like he was hot and uncomfortable in his skin.

"Nothing else?" The paramedic asked. "No medications of any kind?" I shook my head. I felt Kenny twitching underneath my hand.

He nodded. Then looked to the other paramedic, who'd come over and knelt on the other side of Kenny. I could see they were preparing to move him, so I squeezed his hand quickly and got out of the way.

The paramedics lifted him gently onto the stretcher then raised it and wheeled him toward the elevator. They were moving quickly but without panic. As we loaded into the elevator, I grabbed his hand and kissed his forehead. He was sweaty and clammy.

"It's going to be alright," I said. But rather than looking comforted, he just started to do a hyper ventilation type of cry again.

Once we were outside and loaded in the ambulance, the paramedic sat down and looked at me.

"OK," he said. "Now that we're away from the work colleagues, has your husband been taking any drugs or does he use drugs?" I was caught off guard.

"No, no, definitely not," I said.

We are pretty sure it's neurological," he said, "and his signs aren't consistent with a heart attack." He paused. "It could be a stroke, but we'll know more when we get to the hospital."

I looked at Kenny, hooked up to the IV's and monitors, lying pale and clammy on the stretcher. The paramedic was moving around him, checking signs and adjusting things while I huddled in the remaining space in the back of the ambulance trying not to touch anything important.

I'd never been in an ambulance before and it was a surreal feeling to see my 41-year-old husband in the stretcher being rushed to the emergency room. I sat back into the rocking of the truck and tried to tune out the sound of the siren. I kept one hand on his leg. Just touching him made me feel better.

When we arrived at the hospital, his condition was urgent so they got him right into a bed and scanned his brain while I was still filling out the paperwork. Afterwards, I was sitting in the waiting room, waiting, softly crying and trying to focus on my breath. Then a lightbulb went off. His car accident! Kenny had totaled a car three weeks ago on his commute home giving him whiplash. Maybe this had something to do with that?

Maybe this tiny bit of information could save his life, I thought as I rushed up to the intake nurse. A tiny spark of hope bubbled up inside. The nurse listened patiently and said she would pass that information on. Then there was nothing left to do but go back to waiting. Eventually, they called me back into the ER to be with him.

I walked down the hall following the nurse and the green footprints painted on the hospital floor. I kept looking around at the other room, the other families with sick or injured loved ones.

As soon as I walked into the room, I felt my hope die. Kenny looked awful. He was just curled up in a ball on a bed, totally unresponsive. Nurses and doctors were scurrying around, hooking him up to tubes and IVs. They kept saying the word, "ischemic".

When one doctor paused for a moment near me, I said, "What does ischemic mean?"

She paused and looked at me briefly, maybe remembering that I needed to be updated. "We think Kenny has had a stroke," she said. "There are only two ways a stroke happens, either from a blood clot or a bleed on the brain. Ischemic is the medical term for a stroke caused by a blood clot."

The doctor walked around to the side of the bed and took a clipboard from a waiting nurse, looked it over quickly, then walked over to meet me. She sat down on the chair next to me. It squeaked as it slid across the floor.

"We need you to sign off on this waiver," she said, handing it to me. "We would like to administer a drug that will blast any clot out of this system. But we need your permission." I started nodding enthusiastically, but she was still talking. "You need to know, if it turns out there is any bleeding on his brain, he will die instantly. We believe the stroke was caused by a clot, but there's a 10% chance that there is bleeding. So, we need your signature to proceed."

She looked at me expectantly, but didn't rush me. I could tell she wanted to be able to get moving on the treatment but was patiently waiting for me to come to grips with the situation.

I knew there wasn't much time to waste, and she sounded confident and even casual. This was just another Thursday afternoon for them. I decided that a 90% chance of living was good enough odds to save his life. I signed the waiver trusting it was the right decision.

As soon as it had been signed, the doctor nodded to the nurse who started to prepare a syringe. Kenny hadn't moved. He was still curled up on his right side in the fetal position. He looked like a little kid. Helpless and fragile. As we waited, he softly mumbled that the lights were too bright and his head was hurting. Another nurse turned off the lights and I held his hand. I hoped that it was a good sign he was at least communicating.

He didn't move while the drug was going in. I watched him closely, hyper-aware of even the smallest eyelid twitch, but nothing happened. He just lay there, immobile, in an unconscious like state.

The nurse turned to me, "We just have to wait until he wakes up to see if it worked."

"How long will that be?" I asked.

"There's no way to know for sure." She turned to look at me. "You also need to be aware that when he wakes up, there's a high possibility that he won't be able to talk, walk, eat or do certain things. It will just depend on the damage caused by the stroke." I must have looked pretty scared because her voice suddenly got a little softer and kinder. "We'll be able to assess him once until he wakes up. Try not to worry until then."

Now that the immediate danger and rush for help had passed,

I didn't know what to do, but there were plenty of thoughts racing through my brain. When should I call his parents? Is there someone else I should be contacting? Was there something I was supposed to be doing?

I didn't have the answers, so I just waited. I sat still and focused on my breath, naturally my thoughts started going down the rabbit hole of "what-ifs." What if he has massive brain damage? What if I never get to speak to him again? What if he dies?

The feeling of worry was overwhelming, but so was the feeling of being connected to the humanity around me. I was in the Emergency Room and I wasn't the only one in pain. I now had the awareness and understanding that in order to stay calm I needed to re-regulate my dysregulated nervous system. Instead of going into my own ego of fear, I chose to zoom out and let my suffering be a force of presence, compassion and patience.

So, I started singing a song in Sanskrit that I learned at Yoga Teacher Training, "Lokah Samastah Sukhino Bhavantu." It means, "May all beings everywhere be happy and free, and may the thoughts, words and actions of my own life contribute in some way to that happiness and freedom for all." Singing this quietly to myself, repeatedly, allowed my mind to focus and embrace the only thing I could control, my attitude and response to the situation.

With my eyes closed, I started visualizing strength for Kenny and everyone in the hospital to heal, cope and deal. In the hall I'd passed a family with a sick baby. I had seen the drawn, pinched look on the mother's face, and the clenched jaw of the father as they'd clung to each other trying to comfort their wailing child. I sent them love.

I thought of the mom with the son with the strapped arm. He

was still in his school uniform, torn on one side from whatever had happened to cause the injury. He'd padded down the hall barefoot while his mom held onto his sneakers and called out to the nurse. I sent them peace.

I'd seen a daughter with an unconscious elderly mother who'd come in around the same time as Kenny. The mother had been so pale that she'd almost seemed translucent. The daughter was in tears, visibly distraught. She held onto the edge of the hospital bed as the paramedics transferred her mother from the mobile unit to the hospital unit. I could see her knuckles whiten as she clutched the metal bars, but her hands when she touched her mom's face were gentle. I sent them patience.

Sending random strangers loving-kindness was a little thing, but it was the only thing I could do. Kenny's soul was the only one who could decide his outcome. I knew that whatever happened, it was not up to me and life is bigger than me, bigger than just one moment.

That doesn't mean I wasn't scared, there was just a louder, deeper knowing that life is self-correcting, and everything happens for me, not against me. So, I kept singing softly, "Lokah Samastah Sukhino Bhavantu" - focusing on love and faith, and waiting for my love and faith to wake up.

∼

After two hours in the ER, Kenny started to wake. Slowly he began moving and stirring, and to me, it looked like he was coming back to life.

"Babe," I said, holding his hand. "Do you know where you

are?"

"Yes," he said. And at that one word, I breathed a sigh of relief. "Hospital." I felt the tears slide down my cheeks and I kissed him again.

"You seriously scared the shit out of me," I said.

"Sorry babe," he tried a small smile.

Turns out that he knew exactly what had happened, where he was and what was going on. His speech and thinking were coherent and the only physical difference he felt was a pounding headache plus a shaky signature with his right hand.

His brain scan showed scars on both sides of his cerebellum, which meant he had at least one stroke previously in addition to the one that had landed him in the hospital but we have no idea when it could have been. Maybe in his sleep? We'll never know. They also discovered that he has a gene that thickens his blood plus a tiny hole in his heart which exacerbated the problem so they wanted to close it. That was going to be another surgery in a few months and after only five days in the hospital, he was free to go. All he had to do was take a daily low dose aspirin and a few weeks of mandatory physical therapy.

Nothing is permanent, but the universe did not want me to go through everything I'd been through only to lose Kenny two years in. The universe was strategically setting our twin flame journey up for the next stage. We were well past the yearning, meeting, honeymoon and challenges, now we were in the thick of the test phase. Insecurities, traumas, and fears rippled to the surface for the both of us that following year. We entered our Dark Night of the Soul. The chase stage was quickly shadowed by the surrender stage where we dealt with and resolved the murkiness, together. And ever since then we have been in the home stretch. The balance is restored and we continue to facilitate growth for each other. All eight twin flame stages passed in our first three years together.

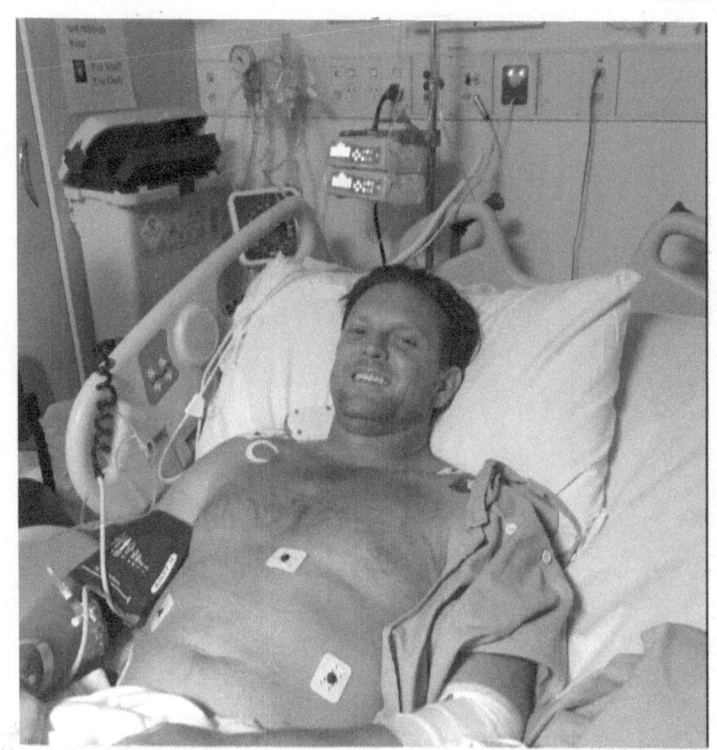

Kenny after stroke - Royal Brisbane Hospital

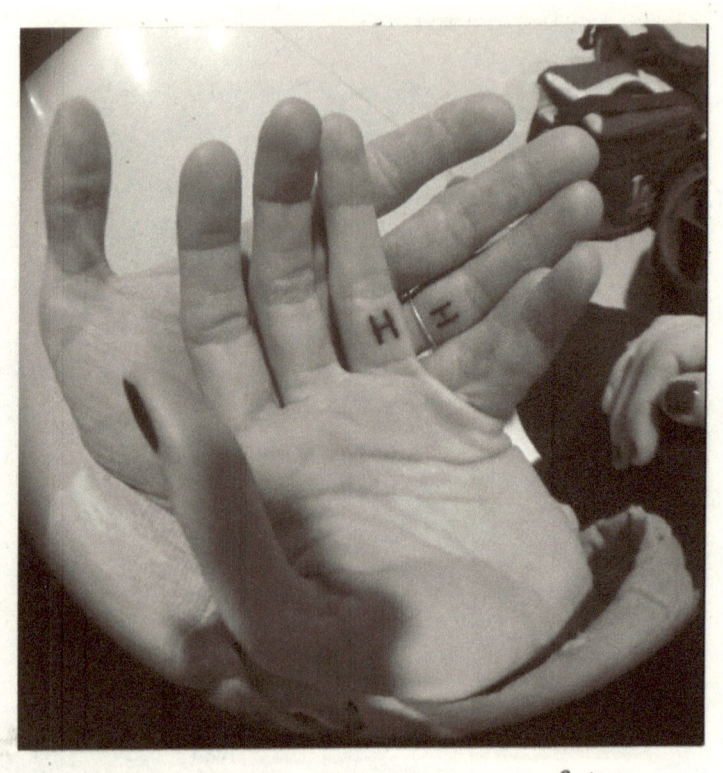

Our tattoos days after the wedding — LAP

Chapter 27

TRUST THE FLAMES

Kenny and I never had a honeymoon, so we created a term called "honey-life." Instead of celebrating each other for a week on some exotic island, we figured, why not celebrate every day? The honey-life is not a whimsical feeling though, yes, most of the time it feels great, but the honey-life is a choice to show up and be real with each other every day. It's challenging and it takes work however it's a safe space where two people are free to be themselves while still evolving together.

After we married, we both tattooed the letter "H" on our ring fingers because we didn't have official rings at the time and it reminds us to strive for the honey-life. The H is not for honey nor Kenny's last name (those are just coincidences). A capital H is two free-standing independent aligned "I's" (individuals) connected by a line (love) in the middle that bolsters their foundation. The H symbolizes that we can be resilient and fulfilled alone, but by supporting each other and meeting halfway, we're stronger and better together. I think of that African proverb, "If you want to go fast, go alone. If you want to go far, go together."

My twin flame journey has brought me to a place of deep love and trust. Travelling it well required Kenny and I to change our own ingrained beliefs about ourselves, our lives and our future. This required us to be more vulnerable, upgrade our emotional language and learn how to deal with conflict so we may have bad moments but we don't have bad days. We have weathered storms and I know with Capable Kenny by my side, anything is possible, including emotional maturity in a partnership. Together life holds more than I could have understood all those years ago.

This journey also helped me heal the relationship with my Mamacita. My grief from her passing was the catalyst to this unexpected adventure and her brave energy has never left me. I'm grateful for everything that we went through. Because of it, I have a deeper capacity to forgive and let go. I focus on what she gifted me instead of what lacked. She empowered me and instilled the courage to trust my internal flames and the fires that life will ignite. I understand that her actions were just a reflection of how she was feeling on the inside at the time. As they say in Alcoholics Anonymous, "We're only as sick as our secrets." She had her own set of traumas, wounds and conditioning. Learning about this with my mom means that I see hardships and adversity as a path to more compassion. I think of it as my compost!

Each challenge is another opportunity to trust the flames and choose courage over comfort. Life is not meant to be flawless or fireless but I have taken a worthwhile journey through the mire and love where I have landed. Plus, I trust the next chapter because I know the author.

A mantra (by yours truly) for when life ignites a fire but you want to *trust the flames* instead of getting engulfed in them.

Thank you, Universe, for showing me where I am not yet free.
Let me use this opportunity to learn,
grow, feel, expand and open.
Allowing, whatever is to come up,
to just be.
Letting go of any attachments, because I know that
nothing is mine to keep.

ACKNOWLEDGEMENTS

Because this book (and anything in my life) could have never come into existence without others

Thank you to my biggest cheerleader, my dance partner, my twin flame, Capable Kenny, I love you and promise to keep you young & wild!

My faja, thank you for being so graciously you. In all of the chaos, you were the calm and have made our lives so much richer. I love you and know that I wouldn't change a thing.

My chief editor, taco-lover, Kristen. Thank you for helping me get this book off the ground, inspiring me to keep going and allowing me to find my own voice.

Elaine and Dionne —Thank you for your professional editing skills, advice and great tips! Shout out to Reedsy.com (for all inspiring writers).

Kat —My 4th street soul sister. You are a gem. Thank you for your impeccable book proposal guidance, edits and all that you have done. Forever grateful.

Alice — My designer genius for the incredible cover as well as our friendship. You are a true north star and this world is a much brighter place with you in it. Keep shining!

Charyln – Thank you for saving the format of my book last minute!

Michelle – My CCF mural artist, thank you for the polaroid idea and thank you for being a friiiieeennnd. Your heart is true, you're a pal and a confident.

Delish – Thank you for all the amazing memoires I will forever cherish. Riiiide safe!

Hayley —My title inspirer and trustee in the chili. Thank you for being a force showing me that it is possible to return to love.

To friends and family whom I bugged for 3.5 years to read and help with ideas, edits and marketing…Thank YOU for your time, patience and honest feedback.

To everyone else who is a vital thread in my life, you know who you are, thank you for the love, support, and authentic connections. I love you more than coconuts!

And to YOU the reader, THANK YOU. Thank you for reading, supporting, sharing and just being YOU.

ABOUT THE AUTHOR

Katie Delimon is a yoga and meditation teacher, Reiki practitioner, retreat facilitator, and author. Her life journey began in New Jersey, and continued on through West Virginia, New York City, and Los Angeles before *love* brought her to Australia. Today she and her twin flame Kenny live along the winding Brisbane River with their Miniature Bullterrier, Shark. Join one of her wellness retreats or mindfulness programs.

katiedelimon.com

@katiedelimon

FREE MINDFULNESS RESOURCES

- **12 Tools to Build Mental Immunity**
  https://katiedelimon.lpages.co

- **The Mindful Method: 4-week Starter Course**
  https://katiedelimon.thinkific.com/courses/Mindful-method-starter-course

- **The Mindful Method: 12-week Mindfulness Course**
  https://katiedelimon.lpages.co/the-mindful-method-waitlist/

www.ingramcontent.com/pod-product-compliance
Lightning Source LLC
Chambersburg PA
CBHW020319010526
44107CB00054B/1902